DOUBLEDAY
CELEBRATES
100 YEARS OF
EXCELLENCE

Also by Thomas Richards
Zero Tolerance

The
Meaning
of
STAR
TREK

THOMAS RICHARDS

DOUBLEDAY
New York London Toronto Sydney Auckland

PUBLISHED BY DOUBLEDAY
a division of Bantam Doubleday Dell Publishing Group, Inc.
1540 Broadway, New York, New York 10036

DOUBLEDAY and the portrayal of an anchor with a dolphin are trademarks
of Doubleday, a division of Bantam Doubleday Dell Publishing Group, Inc.

Book design by Bonni Leon-Berman

This book was not prepared, approved, licensed, or endorsed by any entity
involved in creating or producing the *Star Trek* television series or films.

Library of Congress Cataloging-in-Publication Data

Richards, Thomas, 1956–
The meaning of Star trek / Thomas Richards. — 1st ed.
p.   cm.
1. Star trek, the next generation (Television program) 2. Star Trek
television programs—History and criticism. I. Title.
PN1992.77.S732R5   1997
791.45′72—dc21   97-6845
CIP

ISBN 0-385-48437-2

For Page

CONTENTS

The
Meaning
of
STAR
TREK

INTRODUCTION

There is nothing like *Star Trek*. The voyages of the starship *Enter-prise* take place in an expanding universe of places and peoples. First there were Klingons and Romulans, then Ferengi and Cardassians, then Kaysan and Jem'Hadar. The *Star Trek* universe has grown larger and larger with each new episode and each new series. It seems only a matter of time until all four quadrants of the galaxy will be full of Federation ships making contact with strange new worlds. Of all the universes of science fiction, the *Star Trek* universe is the most varied and extensive, and by all accounts the series is the most popular science fiction ever.

But why *Star Trek*? What is it about this one show, of all the shows on television, that has attracted and sustained audiences for thirty years? Back in the 1970s people used to refer to *Star Trek* fans derisively as "Trekkies," but it seems that *Star Trek* fans have had the last word. The *Star Trek* franchise is now the largest on television. No other series in the history of the medium has proved so supple through so many variations. The original series ran from 1967 to 1969. There was a cartoon version of the original series in 1973–75 with voices of the original stars. A second series, *Star Trek: The Next Generation,* ran from 1987 to 1994, gathering one of the most loyal audiences in television history. Eight movies have been made and more are on the way. Two new and successful *Star Trek* spinoffs, *Star Trek: Deep Space Nine* and *Star Trek: Voyager,* have begun to win over new audiences. Once considered a cult, *Star Trek* is now part of the vocabulary of modern American culture. Just think of all the words and phrases that are now part of our everyday language, words like "phaser" and "warp," phrases like "beam me up" and "space, the final frontier." The crew of an American space shuttle recently posed in Starfleet uniforms, and in some ways it may be that our very idea of space exploration has been shaped more by the series than by recent events. *Star Trek,* it seems, is everywhere.

But hardly anyone has stopped to ask why. Many books cater to *Star Trek* fans, but few take their interests seriously. Encyclopedias covering every aspect of the Federation's universe are issued every few years in new and up-to-date editions. There are detailed technical manuals explaining every piece of technology mentioned in the series. Now you can even buy a grammar book of the Klingon language, complete with tapes recorded by Lieutenant Worf showing you how to pronounce Klingon correctly. But the one thing you cannot find anywhere is a book about what the series means in and of itself. Where does *Star Trek* come from? Why is it so popular? How does it go about creating a coherent world? Literary critics may take literature seriously, but they often look down on popular forms such as television shows. I feel differently. I think the meaning of the series can best be captured by looking at how it successfully creates a coherent universe. Like any great work of art or literature, the *Star Trek* universe has an integrity and a resonance all its own, a completeness unrivaled by any other kind of science fiction, whether movie, television show, or novel. The unique character of the series, taken not as a group of loosely connected stories but as a viable whole, is the subject of this book.

The Meaning of Star Trek looks at the organization of the *Star Trek* universe in its every basic aspect. The basic assumption of this book is the assumption of coherence. I begin by assuming that everything fits together in the *Star Trek* universe, that everything is there for a reason. To take one example, the *Star Trek* universe has a very particular geography. Despite the supposedly infinite nature of the universe, the galaxy in the series is in fact divided into a group of different empires inhabited by different peoples, different dimensions inhabited by different beings, and various uncrossable energy borders. The job of the *Enterprise* is not only to extend these borders but also, and just as importantly, to maintain them through a series of police actions. In an episode of *The Next Generation* called "The Chase" a character accuses Captain Jean-Luc Picard of being "like a Roman centurion off patroling the provinces," ensuring "the maintenance of a dull and bloated Empire." This accusation is only partially true, but it speaks volumes about the organization of the *Star Trek* universe. Again and again we shall see that space in *Star Trek* is anything but empty. Space is full of life which, if not exactly human life, conforms to certain political and social regularities that can be traced out. The chapters of this book look at the organization of the *Star Trek* universe in its essential aspects. One chapter deals with the political structure of the quadrant; another with the psychological structure of the individual character; another with the structure of the stories and myths the series tells; another still with the sense of religion in the series, which, though not exactly conventional, always invokes a certain sense of wonder. "I like to think of the seven years as one big episode," said Michael Dorn, the actor who played Lieutenant Worf during the seven seasons of *The Next Generation,* and in a certain sense, because a small number of themes appear in almost every episode, it is.

The aim of this book, then, is interpretive, not descriptive. In it there is no attempt to cover every character or mention every episode. Instead my emphasis is on the themes and structures basic to the series. In selecting episodes for analysis I have done more than pick my favorites. As everyone knows, the series is full of bad episodes as well as good ones, but seen from the perspective of a critic, these bad episodes can often tell us as much about the organization of the *Star Trek* universe as the good ones can. A masterful episode like "Darmok" may contain in concentrated form all the essential themes of the series, but no less important is "Skin of Evil," an episode vital to the series because it is the only episode in which a major character, Lieutenant Tasha Yar, dies. Throughout this book I have done my best to single out representative episodes. Behind each of these are often dozens of corroborating examples. Summaries of all the episodes can be found in *The Star Trek Compendium* or in *The Star Trek Encyclopedia,* but unlike this book, those books do not attempt to ask what the series means.

Though interpretative, *The Meaning of Star Trek* deals with the *Star Trek* universe in its own terms. This book does not import critical terminology from anywhere else to explain things peculiar to *Star Trek*. *Star Trek* is great because it creates a coherent universe in which its various parts fit together beautifully. The aim of this book is to plumb the mechanics of that fit, to understand how it is put together and why. *Star Trek* is not an allegory of anything, not an allegory of our own political world or of any preceding political world, nor is it an allegory derived from any literary model. *Star Trek* must be taken on its own terms, for therein lies its greatness. Any great work of literature is great because it somehow supersedes that which has come before, and *Star Trek* is no exception to this rule. It utterly supersedes both in depth and breadth the science fictions which have come before it. There really is nothing like *Star Trek,* and as we shall see, there are dozens of discernible reasons why the series is the most popular science fiction ever devised.

The Meaning of Star Trek dwells in greatest length on the episodes

4

of *The Next Generation,* the second of the *Star Trek* series. I do so not because I like the cast or stories better, but because the second series represents Gene Roddenberry's vision of the Federation in its full maturity. In *The Making of Star Trek* Roddenberry relates how studio pressures forced him to alter his original vision. He had to rewrite many episodes to insert many action scenes in which Kirk is made to act like the star of a 1960s cowboy show. Those episodes of the original series with the least physical combat are often closest to Roddenberry's original version, which always stresses diplomacy over military action. Though the original *Star Trek* series is now seen as the classic, *The Next Generation* is in fact truer to Roddenberry's original vision of the series. He wanted to use many of the features of the second series in the first but was simply not allowed to. In 1987 Roddenberry was given free rein for the first time in his career, and the result is a far fuller vision of the Federation than seen in the first series. Classic *Star Trek* is the rough draft of *The Next Generation. The Next Genertion* is the mature and unimpeded vision of Gene Roddenberry, the place where all the original elements of his *Star Trek* vision achieve their full development. It is enormously difficult to create a viable fictional world set at some point in the distant future, and most science fiction, though immensely imaginative, fails in its effort to do so. *Star Trek* succeeded fully only on the second try, but even then the series did not come fully into its own until the third season of *The Next Generation,* that is, until after nearly two hundred episodes and five movies had been made. Like any maturing artist, Roddenberry saw deeper into his vision as he lived longer within the world he had created.

The *Star Trek* universe is thus a very vast universe indeed, a universe thirty years in the making. It may have begun as the vision of one man, Gene Roddenberry, but viewed in a larger perspective, the series must be seen as a collective achievement, the result of years of collaboration between many different writers, directors, actors, producers, and designers. Though Gene Roddenberry was certainly responsible for the general "look" of the series, Roddenberry was an idea man who knew that he needed to solicit the help of others to fill in the blank spaces on the Federation map. Many science fictions have interesting ideas behind them, but *Star Trek* pays very close attention to the details, from the systems of rank and color-coding of the uniforms to the layout of the sets and the design of the ship models and prosthetics. The truth is that it is very hard for a single individual to imagine an entire social world. Large novels aiming at representing entire societies tend to be intensely realistic, dealing in all instances with actually existing societies, and very few works of science fiction succeed in creating a rounded world worthy of a realistic novel. This is why science fiction novels tend to be serial in form; it takes more than one attempt to create a rounded future world. Most science fiction is unsuccessful because it takes on too much. *Star Trek* manages to amass an incredibly coherent universe of small details over many years only through the efforts of many, many people. Unlike many literary genres, science fiction is well suited to the efforts of many discrete contributors, which is why the screen versions of science fiction classics are often so much more fully realized than the books themselves, which suffer from the limits of an individual creator trying to imagine and inhabit a completely imaginary world.

The conditions of television also favored the series. The *Star Trek* movies can often be very bad, favoring special effects over story and dwelling overmuch on the ship itself rather than its crew, as in the famous scene in *Star Trek—The Motion Picture* where the camera lingers on the image of the reconstructed *Enterprise* for nearly ten minutes. In a way, television gave *Star Trek* a great economy of focus. Too many science fiction films are exercises in special effects. The budgetary constraints of a typical *The Next Generation* episode—about a million dollars per episode—had the effect of shifting the focus away from technology and toward character, plot, story, and myth. It was for budgetary considerations that some of the best episodes of the series were shot without leaving the set of the *Enterprise*. There will never be anything in a televised *Star Trek* episode like the great final attack on the Death Star in *Star Wars*. Visuals in the series are mostly static, simply establishing the scene. Publicity stills from *Star Wars* do not do justice to the film, in which the whole idea is motion and action. In *Star Trek*, rather, special effects have the sense of being composed, frames for human activity like the backdrop on a stage. The first two series are full of shots showing the *Enterprise* orbiting lovely colorful planets, red and yellow and blue and green. The *Enterprise* is at her most magnificent when shot dead still, facing a Romulan Warbird or a Klingon Bird of Prey. The *Enterprise* and its many technologies are preeminently a stage set for human concerns and activities. A gray *Enterprise* was chosen because the designer, Matt Jeffries, wanted the starship to have "a relatively plain surface, so that we could throw different colors on it, depending on the story line." Similarly, in the hour-long format of commercial television, a drama has to be broken down into five acts to allow for the insertion of commercial breaks. The peculiar constraints of television do not detract from the series. Rather, they helped provide the series not only with a distinct visual iconography, but also with the five-act dramatic structure basic to all Western theater.

This book is not a history of science fiction. Partly this is because the history of science fiction has already been written by a great science fiction writer, Brian Aldiss, in *Billion Year Spree: The True History of Science Fiction* (1973). (The revised edition of this book won a Hugo Award in 1986). But mostly this is because *Star Trek* is that one rarity: a creation that transcends its point of origin. Gene Roddenberry was raised on 1940s and 1950s science fiction books, 1950s science fiction movies, and 1960s television shows, but the reason he created *Star Trek* is that he was able to see that science fiction could be more, much more, than it had been in the past. In a great many ways, the *Star Trek* universe owes a lot more to early science fiction writers like Jules Verne and H. G. Wells than to later writers like Isaac Asimov and Ray Bradbury. These Victorian writers believed in progress. They believed the world was going to get better, not worse. Certainly one reason why *Star Trek* is so much more popular than any other science fiction, running now in four series and eight movies, is that the series gives us an optimistic picture of the future. In the *Star Trek* future there is no poverty, hunger, discrimination, or disease. You have to go back a long way in science fiction to find such optimism. *Flash Gordon* and *Star Wars* show a world torn between good and evil. *Neuromancer* and *Johnny Mnemonic* show a world overwhelmed by crime and cynicism. Gene Roddenberry was a rarity, a creator of modern science fiction who continued to believe that science would ultimately right all the wrongs of the world. He deliberately set his series apart from all other science fiction, giving us the greatest achievement of the genre, the *Star Trek* universe. This book will show how that universe is put together, and why.

Chapter One

CONTACT
and
CONFLICT

A space station turning to a Richard Strauss waltz. A small ship making its approach to the station like a partner in a dance. For me the most visually remarkable moment in science fiction has always been the space ballet in Stanley Kubrick's *2001: A Space Odyssey* (1968). In this film Kubrick shows the station, shaped like a double wheel, spinning in place as it orbits the earth. The station does not dominate the screen. It is a small island of life in the vast quiet desolation of space. As Kubrick sees it, the technology of human beings clearly pales in comparison with the earth, sun, moon, and stars. Human beings are by no means the masters of the universe. They move around in it slowly, hampered by weightlessness, trapped in space suits, and hooked up to respirators. In many ways *2001: A Space Odyssey* accords with what astronauts of all nations have been telling us for years: that space is a cold and empty place.

In *Star Trek* space is anything but empty. In all of *Star Trek* there is nothing like the space ballet scene in Kubrick's movie. A comparable scene from the first *Star Trek* movie makes a clear point of comparison. In this movie Captain James T. Kirk and his reunited crew are shown approaching the revamped *Enterprise*. The space station and the starships fill the screen. Human figures are strongly in evidence. Kirk and the crew are seen watching from windows. The scene reflects the general attitude of the series toward space: at every turn *Star Trek* is full of the presence of life in outer space. The desolate quality of outer space imagined by Kubrick and experienced by our astronauts plays a relatively minor role in the series. Instead space serves as a landscape, beautiful and distinctly pictorial, a background for human activity and intensely human concerns. The most visually memorable scenes in *Star Trek* take place on particular planets or on board the *Enterprise* itself. From time to time the crew of the *Enterprise* confronts purely empty space, but there is nothing in the series to rival the space ballet of *2001: A Space Odyssey*.

Rather, the *Star Trek* universe is a noisy and populated place. Stanley Kubrick calls his movie "a space *Odyssey*," and true to his title, he gives us a vision of space like that of Homer's poem the *Odyssey*. The *Odyssey* tells the story of a single hero, Odysseus, trying to get home after fighting in the Trojan War. But on his way back Odysseus gets lost in the Mediterranean Sea. Kubrick bases his story of a lone astronaut lost in space on Homer's story of a single man in a small ship lost alone at sea. Though *Star Trek* certainly has some elements of the *Odyssey* in it (I will be looking at them later), the series more often resembles the world of Homer's other epic, the *Iliad.* Homer's *Iliad* is an epic about diplomacy and the uneasy rivalries of different races, the Greeks and the Trojans, who fight the Trojan War on the coastal plains of what is now Turkey. The *Iliad* shows the Mediterranean to be not an empty and desolate world but a populated world full of wars, rivalries, and divine and human passions. In many ways *Star Trek* is "a space *Iliad,*" not "a space *Odyssey.*" The series shows a Federation of planets slowly expanding into the outer reaches of the universe, where, more often than not, it confronts not emptiness and desolation but a bewildering array of other forms of life.

The *Star Trek* universe, then, is full of races of different kinds of beings. This may seem a very simple assumption, but it is not an assumption that every work of science fiction makes. Isaac Asimov's *Foundation* series imagines a future in which human beings colonize a galaxy that turns out to be empty and inhospitable. *Star Trek* begins with the fact and problem not just of *other life* in the universe but of *compatible life* in the universe and never takes it for granted. Space is never completely alien. In all of *Star Trek* there is nothing like the scenario depicted in the movie *Alien,* which shows a space freighter drifting out of reach from human contact, faced only with the frightening otherness of a completely malignant non-human being. Even when a starship is magically transported to a different part of the galaxy, as in the newest series, *Star Trek: Voyager,* space turns out to be very much inhabited and full of M-class planets. The map of the galaxy seen in the series shows a great swirling wheel of stars divided into territory controlled by Klingons, Romulans, Cardassians, Ferengi, and Borg. The universe is full of empires old and new and the Federation and its colonists are always getting into trouble with them. Many of its best episodes deal with the conflict of cultures resulting from the Federation's relentless expansion into outer space.

The *Star Trek* stories of contact and conflict with other species typically follow three different scenarios. In the first scenario the Federation is considerably more powerful than a primitive or underdeveloped society. The *Enterprise* and its crew are mistaken for gods and are often drawn into rituals playing out the death of a god as part of some sort of religious festival. The first *Star Trek* series almost always draws on this scenario of first contact, which places the crew of the *Enterprise* in the position of explorers during the our own age of discovery in the sixteenth and seventeenth centuries. In the second scenario the Federation finds itself at rough parity with the forces of other empires. Relations with the Klingons, Romulans, and Cardassians follow this pattern. The second *Star Trek* series tends to specialize in these kinds of plots, where interstellar tension is lessened through the best efforts of the Federation's master diplomat, Captain Jean-Luc Picard. In the third scenario the Federation is inferior and its very existence is threatened. The best movies and novels in the science fiction genre, from H. G. Wells's *The War of the Worlds* to Arthur C. Clarke's *Childhood's End* to the movie *Alien,* consistently follow this scenario, which dislocates the position of human beings in the universe, and *Star Trek* is no exception. The story of first contact with the Borg, told in a trilogy of remarkable episodes, may well be ranked among the greatest achievements of science fiction.

1

In *Star Trek* the central experience of space travel is the experience of encounter. Given the state of our knowledge of outer space, this is a necessarily fictional encounter. But the series does not give us a purely fictional view of prospective life in outer space. Like most other science fiction, *Star Trek* fills the void of our own knowledge by drawing on the historical experience of earth's own age of exploration. In the sixteenth and seventeenth centuries explorers like Columbus, Magellan, and Cortés ventured out into what they too called "strange new worlds." Not in one case was the land empty. The new world they explored was very much an inhabited world full of ancient civilizations and established traditions. The first explorers were as much invaders as explorers, and the Spanish went so far as to call their explorers *conquistadors,* a Spanish word meaning "conquerors." Historically there is no such thing as exploration for exploration's sake. Exploration usually leads to empire, and empire leads to war.

Gene Roddenberry was very aware how, in our own history, exploration has often been little more than a pretext for conquest and empire. He made the Federation into an organization acting first and foremost on one general principle. This principle is the Prime Directive. The Prime Directive mandates that Starfleet personnel are prohibited from interfering with the normal development of any society they may encounter. From the outset Roddenberry's intention in creating the Prime Directive was very clear: the central principle of Starfleet effectively prevents it from establishing an empire in outer space. In his book *The Making of Star Trek* he remarks that he did not want the Federation to wipe out the Aztecs all over again. He was referring to the brutal conquest of the Americas by the Spanish in the sixteenth century. Roddenberry often said he created the Prime Directive because he wanted the Federation to act as a corrective to this bloody history of exploration. But not as a simple or facile corrective. Today we often blame the Spanish for slaughtering the Aztecs, but Roddenberry would typically ask a more penetrating question. What if, in exploring space, *we* were to come upon a society founded on human sacrifice? In "A Taste of Armageddon" Kirk finds a society founded on periodic executions of its members. In "Half a Life" Picard deals with a society that kills anyone over sixty. The great achievement of *Star Trek* is not the creation of a principle in theory but the staging of a variety of circumstances testing it in practice.

The Prime Directive is by no means a rigid principle. The way it is applied almost always depends on the balance of power. The more the balance is tilted toward the Federation, the more important the principle becomes. The episodes exploring the meaning of the Prime Directive almost always deal with a society or being perceived as less powerful than the Federation. The Federation is capable of acting with considerable restraint when dealing with underdeveloped societies. But the Directive completely disappears in a contest of equals. The Federation actively spies on the Cardassians. Relations with the Klingons are full of intrigue. Ambassador Spock undertakes a mission to Romulus which, though well intended in its design to bring about the reunification of Romulus and Vulcan, deliberately intervenes in Romulan internal affairs, an outright violation of the Prime Directive. And with the Borg the principle itself comes very close to being reversed. At one point, after losing thirty-seven starships and eleven thousand crew in an all-out battle with the Borg, Picard seriously contemplates a plan to eradicate the entire race. He decides against it, but in a later episode an admiral from Starfleet Command goes so far as to reprimand him for not committing this act of genocide, an act which, if carried out, would have constituted the ultimate violation of the Prime Directive.

The Prime Directive has a further problem. Not only is it easy to violate the Prime Directive; in fact, it is hard not to violate it. Almost any action taken by Starfleet, ranging from tentative exploration to outright colonization, is by definition a violation of the Prime Directive. This is through no fault of any starship captain. It is because the Prime Directive is not only an unattainable ideal but also a scientific impossibility. Behind the Prime Directive is the idea that it is possible to observe a society without actually affecting it. Seen in this way, the Prime Directive constitutes a violation of one of *Star Trek*'s favorite scientific principles: the Heisenberg Uncertainty Principle. The Heisenberg Uncertainty Principle states that observers always interfere with the things that they are observing. Even a hidden observer creates a disturbance. The interference may be small or it may be great, but it is everpresent and it can be measured. If we believe Heisenberg (as the series does), we must admit that the Prime Directive is founded on a scientific impossibility. Maintaining a perfect distance is simply not possible in a universe where all actions, however remote, have consequences. No observation is or can be neutral. Observers are necessarily participants. Wherever Starfleet goes in the galaxy, it must act to limit the damage inevitably caused by its own powers of observation. Violating the Prime Directive is thus a matter not of principle but of degree.

But there are violations and there are violations. In "The Drumhead" retired Admiral Norah Satie threatens to put Picard on trial for violating the Prime Directive no less than nine times. Lieutenant Worf immediately jumps to his defense, saying, "Captain Picard did the only thing he could," proceeding to give the court various details about how Picard acted to save the ship. In this particular episode, which I will go over later, the judge is discredited and Picard never actually comes up for trial. But the accusation she makes has real resonance. Picard does violate the Prime Directive at least nine times, and each time he has a perfectly good, perfectly sane reason for doing so. Each time he is faced with the Prime Directive, he makes partly an abstract choice, based on principle, and partly a very personal choice, based on a particular situation and on the basic welfare of his ship and crew. In no situation does Picard, or Kirk before him, choose the Prime Directive over the survival of his crew. What both of them do make are a series of compromise choices, some better than others, designed to minimize the Federation's impact on the galaxy. They still make many mistakes, but from the time of Kirk to the time of Picard, the Federation tries to learn from these mistakes and perfect the application of its own Directive, an application which, due to the flaws in the principle itself, can never really be perfect.

The first series is full of outright violations of the Prime Directive. In this James T. Kirk remains true to his middle name, Tiberius, a first-century Roman emperor known to history mostly as a man who did whatever he wanted, whenever he felt like it, no matter what the consequences. To be fair, Kirk and his crew often have to spend a lot of time repairing damage done to other planets by prior Federation violations of the Prime Directive. In "Patterns of Force" a Federation historian has set up a social system based on Nazi Germany. In "A Piece of the Action" someone on a Federation ship left behind a book about gangsters in 1920s Chicago, and a planet has proceeded to model itself on it. But in many other episodes Kirk and his crew do the damage themselves. A particularly common plot found in the original series is the "trouble in utopia" plot. In this scenario Kirk stumbles on a peaceful but totalitarian world. The closer he looks at this world, the less he likes it, and in the end he can hardly restrain himself from acting on behalf of human freedom and overthrowing the government. In "The Return of the Archons" he disrupts an ordered society simply because it is a little too authoritarian for his taste. In "A Private Little War" he starts supplying arms to a tribal people on a primitive planet. Usually in these kinds of episodes Kirk justifies taking action because he must save his ship or a crew member. But in many other episodes his actions amount to a deliberative violation of the Directive. In "The Omega Glory" Kirk finds that the Klingons have been supplying one faction on a warring world with new arms and new technologies. In this situation Kirk has many courses of action open to him. He could remove the weaponry; he could confront the Klingons in space; he could even withdraw. But he chooses to supply the other faction with equal armaments. He acts not to preserve the Prime Directive but to uphold the balance of power in the galaxy. As we shall see shortly, this is the perhaps the most characteristic action undertaken by Starfleet vessels. In *The Next Generation* as well as in the original series the Prime Directive often pales in importance to the balance of power.

There is, however, one mitigating circumstance deserving our sympathy. It has to do with the scope of the Prime Directive. The Prime Directive is, after all, a law, and laws rarely remain in force beyond their place of jurisdiction. But the Federation promulgated the Prime Directive to be much more than a law binding in Federation space. The Prime Directive is intended to be binding *anywhere in the galaxy*. This makes it unique among laws, for it is a law whose application is not restricted to a particular territory. On our own planet areas not falling within any legal jurisdiction have a history of degenerating into complete anarchy. The frontier is by definition a place beyond the pale of civilization. The conditions of the frontier rarely allow the usual conventions of law and diplomacy to remain intact and functioning. Most Westerns, for example, deal with the improvised justice peculiar to frontier conditions, showing crude attempts to maintain law and order where none exists formally. In the same way James Tiberius Kirk has to uphold the Prime Directive under cowboy conditions where he is often the only law there is. Under ideal circumstances the Prime Directive would be difficult to enforce, but under these frontier conditions keeping to the Directive often requires a near-heroic act of restraint, an act which Kirk, for one, is not always capable of. There is a good reason why Kirk and his crew seem very frequently to be transported to the Old West. Space is indeed the final frontier, and the Prime Directive always has to be enforced under frontier conditions. As we have seen, these conditions make for a very poor record of implementing Starfleet's General Order Number One.

The second series certainly improves on the record of the first. But in *The Next Generation* violations of the Prime Directive persist. These are less due to the sloppy application of the principle seen in the first series. They are due more to the internal fault of the principle itself, that is, to its faulty premise that it is possible for observers to remain fully external to a situation they are observing. In "Justice" Wesley Crusher visits a pleasure planet and is sentenced to death for some minor infraction, and the *Enterprise* must intervene to save him. In "Pen Pals" Lieutenant Commander Data exchanges messages with a little girl on a distant planet, then comes to her rescue when he learns that her planet is dying. In "The Masterpiece Society" the *Enterprise* saves a planet from an asteroid only to find that it has irrevocably altered its social fabric. In each of these cases the crew members were not aware that they were violating the Prime Directive at the time they were violating it. Few of these incidents could have been prevented except by avoiding contact entirely, and given that Starfleet's basic mission is to explore the universe, they probably could not have been avoided at all.

The situation is very different in "Who Watches the Watchers?" In this episode Starfleet has deliberately set up an anthropological research station on Mintaka Three, which has a primitive culture that has no knowledge of outside worlds. A few Mintakans stumble into it. One of the Mintakans suffers radiation burns and is beamed to sickbay, where, on awakening, he sees Captain Picard and realizes that he is the one in charge. Returned to the planet, he tells the people in his village that he has been healed by a god called "The Picard." In the end Picard himself has to beam down and confront the Mintakans, trying to reason with them. One of the Mintakans points a bow at Picard, telling the others that the arrow will bounce off him because he is a god. But when the Mintakan fires, the arrow lodges in Picard's shoulder and he falls to the ground. The spell is broken, at least for now; the Mintakans begin to realize that the crew of the *Enterprise* are people, not gods. The damage done by the anthropologists has been undone, or so they hope.

The position of the anthropologist comes under close scrutiny in this episode. To do the job right, any anthropologist must observe a society over a relatively long period of time. Anthropologists routinely spend years in the field; some spend decades. Anthropologists are observers who live among the people they observe, and they regularly face some of the problems we have already seen in interpreting and implementing the Prime Directive. They put themselves in an essentially superior position. They refuse to restrain their own curiosity. And most of all, they put themselves in the impossible position of the observer who struggles to avoid changing the things being observed. All anthropology is by definition a violation of the Prime Directive, and at one point in the episode one of the anthropologists makes a revealing suggestion to Picard. The damage has been done, he tells him. The Prime Directive has already been violated. So he might as well start "giving them guidelines, letting them know what the Overseer expects of them." This is observation gone awry, for this anthropologist will do anything to allow his studies to continue, even deliberately and irrevocably altering the course of the society that he is observing. In "Who Watches the Watchers?" the anthropologists may have enjoyed the protection of a kind of one-way mirror, but when that mirror cracks, they blithely interfere with a society in the most basic way possible, by altering its fundamental structure of religious belief. The impact of anthropology on Mintaka Three is nearly catastrophic, and the anthropologists on Mintaka Three offer something like a nightmare scenario of Prime Directive violation: Starfleet setting itself up as a god ruling over technologically inferior cultures.

The way Picard averts catastrophe is by demonstrating his mortality to the Mintakans. Seeing that the Mintakans do not believe him when he tells them, "I am a man, nothing more," he invites a bowman to take aim and fire. The arrow flies from the bow and strikes Picard in the shoulder, hurling him to the ground. This seems to do the trick, for once he is wounded, the Mintakans begin to approach him without reverence or fear. The problem here, however, is that the killing or maiming of a god is perhaps the most deeply rooted of primitive rituals. Primitive societies kill a god as an act of faith so that the god can prove his power by staging his own resurrection. For a moment in "Who Watches the Watchers?", "The Picard" lies in agony, clearly mortal. Picard does not magically extract the arrow from his shoulder, and the Mintakans now appear to regard him as mortal. But the question remains: What happens once the *Enterprise* leaves and the incident with Picard enters Mintakan mythology? The episode plays out only the first half of the death of the god, the mime of his mortality. But it entirely omits the second half, the restoration of the god in all his terrifying godhead. A final scene of the episode shows Picard on the surface of the planet, miraculously restored to near-normal state by Dr. Beverly Crusher in sickbay. There is simply no knowing whether the Mintakans will be able to accept the knowledge of a powerful yet mortal being. The episode makes clear the mythmaking tendencies of a primitive society, and there is a distinct possibility that the Mintakans will take this particular myth to its usual conclusion, restoring "The Picard" to his status as god. There has only been a single instance of contact between the Mintakans and the Federation; without further instances of contact, reversion to their mythic frame of mind is certainly a very real possibility.

But the damage has been done, most of it in the name of simple observation. One of the place-names used in the episode points clearly to the violence hidden in every act of observation. In "Who Watches the Watchers?" the anthropologists live in a station everyone calls the "duck blind," a very revealing choice of a name for an observation post. A duck blind is a hidden position in a marsh or a forest from which hunters shoot ducks. The hunters get to see the ducks, but the ducks cannot see the hunters, who pick the ducks off one by one. The duck blind is used here as a metaphor for the violence implicit in every act of observation. The duck blind is an observation post that is also a killing post. In "Who Watches the Watchers?" the implication is that the observers in the Mintaka duck blind are by no means neutral. They are interested observers who carry within them the potential for great destruction. This history of anthropology is full of examples of anthropologists who discover a society only to have that discovery exploited for political or economic purposes. After years of isolation, these societies can often break down under the sudden pressure of intense scrutiny. This happened to the Tupí in Brazil. Frequently, as in the case of the Guaraní in Paraguay, they are wiped out before they have a chance to join the larger world community. Something of this fate may await the Mintakans, whose development was irrevocably altered by the Federation anthropologists sitting in their duck blind. At the end of the episode the *Enterprise* leaves Mintaka in order to minimize damage to the culture of the planet. We never do find out what happens to the Mintakans, but the episode's standing metaphor for observation, the duck blind, gives a clear and very harsh assessment: every act of observation is an act of force, and often, by extension, an act of violence. The need to use a cloaking device (here it is called a holographic generator) should itself be a tip-off, for in *Star Trek* cloaking devices are a technology employed by untrustworthy species and peoples.

The episode does a good job of highlighting the shortcomings of Starfleet's system of self-regulation, but in the end its very title asks the most piercing question of all. Who is watching the watchers, anyway? The answer is that the watchers are supposed to be watching themselves, regulating their conduct according to the Federation's central principle, the Prime Directive. In principle the Prime Directive is supposed to be helping the watchers watch themselves. In practice, though, nobody is watching the watchers but themselves. The Prime Directive clearly states that primitive cultures are not to be interfered with, but in practice the members of Starfleet are always looking for loopholes in their own law. The anthropologists in "Who Watches the Watchers?" must have thought that they would be safely invisible behind their cloaking device, but when the device failed, they forever changed the self-awareness of the society they were observing. A primitive society exists in relative isolation. But a society is "underdeveloped" only when it becomes aware that there are more privileged societies elsewhere in the universe. Starfleet routinely transforms primitive societies into underdeveloped ones by making them aware of what they do not have, then by proceeding to withhold these things from them under the rubric of the Prime Directive. A primitive society can at least enjoy its own isolation. But an underdeveloped society is a society that is painfully aware that there are others in the universe who are much better off, who enjoy a standard of living that is simply unattainable to them. "Who Watches the Watchers?" ends with Picard telling the Mintakans that they will have to wait thousands of years to reap the benefits of a society and culture such as the Federation's. He then leaves the planet to meditate on its newfound sense of inferiority. The Mintakans will never be the same. Now they will consider themselves to be an underdeveloped society, wanting in things which they now know for certain exist in profusion somewhere else.

To be fair, the Federation sometimes does better in upholding the Prime Directive than it does in "Who Watches the Watchers?" In "Justice" it manages to at least appear to respect local laws and customs. But in no case is a Federation intervention completely benign. Contact always involves conflict, and this conflict can be particularly damaging in cases of first contact, as in "Who Watches the Watchers?" But we can hardly fault Picard and his crew for failing to uphold an unattainable ideal. If a diplomat were to observe the Prime Directive to the letter, there would be little opportunity for any contact between species because the only way to avoid damaging contact and conflict with other species would be to cease exploration altogether. The *Enterprise* is on a diplomatic mission, and the aim of diplomacy is not observation but intervention. Diplomacy always involves contact, negotiation, and compromise. And there are times when diplomacy breaks down. The Federation can always stand on its own against cultures like the Mintakans, but fidelity to the Prime Directive often slips away in the *Star Trek* universe, where not all the societies the *Enterprise* contacts exist at a lesser stage of development. There are Klingons, Romulans, and Cardassians to contend with. More than anything else, the *Star Trek* universe is a universe of equals, full of cultures at technological parity with the Federation. Contact with these cultures leads to a very different kind of conflict, conflict regulated by a balance of power.

2

The Federation is not the only going concern in the galaxy. The Federation is the galaxy's only "federation," that is, its only voluntary union of worlds. It is surrounded by societies calling themselves empires and acting out of all the standard motives for imperial expansion. These societies provide us with a long list of the usual justifications given for building an empire. The Ferengi are in it for wealth. The Klingons are in it for honor. The Cardassians and the Romulans for power. Each of these societies is the technological equal of the Federation. Without a universe full of equals capable of challenging the Federation, the Prime Directive would be just another version of the old idea of the white man's burden, the idea that one race must bear the burden of governing all others. Some episodes of the original series come very close to endorsing this idea that the Federation should be an invisible and benign power. In *The Next Generation,* however, the Federation inhabits a universe of equals in which every action is likely to provoke an equal and opposite reaction.

The shape of the galaxy has changed markedly from the time of the original series to the time of *The Next Generation.* Several times we learn that in the twenty-third century of James T. Kirk only 4 percent of the galaxy has been mapped. The figure jumps to 17 percent in the twenty-fourth century of Jean-Luc Picard. This may still seem like only a small fraction of the galaxy as a whole, but it represents an increase of over 400 percent. Indeed the galaxy of *The Next Generation* is a much more crowded place. Despite all the time the *Enterprise* spends going off into uncharted regions of space, not once in hundreds of episodes is the *Enterprise* completely "lost in space." Every episode begins with a captain's log entry pinpointing date and exact location. Even when the *Enterprise* gets sucked into a wormhole or conveyed by Q to some remote region of space, the computer always manages to tell the crew members where they are. The period of intensive exploration seems mostly to have coincided with the original series. The Federation of *The Next Generation* has settled into a period of consolidating explored space. In most episodes the crew of the *Enterprise* deals with known enemies or with unknown anomalies that happen to have ventured into Federation space. The *Enterprise* only rarely leaves Federation territory, and then only under the gravest of circumstances. Though space is infinite and the *Enterprise* is supposedly exploring it, it turns out the Federation is hemmed in on all sides by hostile cultures, neutral zones, and uncrossable energy barriers.

Some of these cultures have the ring of familiarity. The Romulans and the Klingons both have clear analogues in our own ancient history. Instead of ancient Romans we get aliens from a planet called Romulus. Instead of barbarians we get Klingons (the original Greek word for "barbarian" can be best translated into English as something like "kling" or "klang," referring to the strange sounds foreigners make when they speak). The Romulans organize their fleet of starships like a Roman legion and call their admirals centurions. The Klingons belong to a heroic society whose costume and code of honor mimics the Germanic tribesmen the Romans fought on their German borders in the first few centuries A.D. The series even makes the two into implacable enemies, just as the Romans and barbarians were. The inner workings of these cultures are the subject of many episodes of *The Next Generation.* But the more we know about them, the more sympathetic they become and the less effective they are as potential enemies of the Federation. The producers of *The Next Generation* must have sensed this when they introduced a new race that became the major nemesis of the Federation, the Cardassians.

We first meet the Cardassians in "The Wounded." Typically, as with the Klingons and Romulans, there is no exact moment of first contact. First contact is an experience reserved for underdeveloped or completely nonhuman cultures. Contact with equals is immediately an experience of competition, and the Prime Directive seems to be rendered null and void. In this episode a renegade Federation ship under Captain Benjamin Maxwell has ventured into Cardassian space and is destroying Cardassian ships and stations. Starfleet is desperately trying to maintain the balance of power in the region and is willing to sacrifice Maxwell, a war hero, to preserve the peace. When the *Enterprise* finally catches up with Maxwell's ship, the *Phoenix,* Maxwell beams on board and tells Picard that the Cardassians are using a science station in the Cuellar system as a cover for a military transport station. To preserve the treaty and to prevent war, Picard places Maxwell under arrest and escorts his renegade ship back to Federation space.

Maxwell may be a renegade, but throughout the episode he acts in accordance with a certain system of values. In "The Wounded" Picard is forced to cooperate with Gul Macet, his equal and counterpart among the Cardassians. There is a grudging respect between them as they agree that heroic renegades such as Benjamin Maxwell are out of place in the twenty-fourth century. "It's vengeance he's after," says Macet after talking with Transporter Chief Miles O'Brien, who tells him how Maxwell once witnessed a Cardassian attack on Setlik Three. Working together, they manage to track Maxwell down and talk him out of destroying a Cardassian supply ship. Just before he gives up, Maxwell sings this song, which runs like a refrain through "The Wounded":

The Minstrel-Boy to the war is gone.
In the ranks of death you'll find him;
His father's sword he has girded on,
And his wild harp hung behind him.
"Land of song!" said the warrior-bard,
"Though all the world betrays thee,
One sword, at least, thy rights shall guard,
One faithful harp shall praise thee!"

The song is a traditional Irish ballad called *The Minstrel-Boy*. Its theme is the inadequacy of an old heroic code in dealing with situations posed by a modern political world. The boy in the song goes to a futile and lonely death as the last warrior in the world. Alone among all the species in *Star Trek*, only the Klingons still subscribe to a similar heroic code upholding the values of honor, loyalty, and courage. But again and again in *Star Trek* the Klingons come very close to destroying themselves. They can barely manage their own affairs. Their science is flawed. Their home world is a hive of personal rivalries inflamed by tensions between warring clans. Lieutenant Worf acts in characteristic Klingon fashion when he recommends the aggressive posture of attack in nearly every episode. As viewers we learn to respect Worf's nobility, but we also notice that Captain Picard almost never takes his advice. If he had his way, Worf's heroic code would almost certainly have destroyed the *Enterprise* a long time ago. The Klingons' position in the galaxy is eroding; they belong not to the future but to the past. Like Worf and the rest of the Klingons, Captain Benjamin Maxwell represents a vanishing way of life. He is like the minstrel boy in the Irish song he sings, dying in support of a heroic code that no longer reflects a contemporary reality.

The Cardassians and the Federation live in a different kind of political universe, a universe ruled by the dictates of the balance of power. At different times in our own world history a working balance of power has involved as few as two or as many as ten major powers. But in all cases the balance of power presupposes that no one nation has the ability to fully subdue another. Such a situation rarely comes into being very quickly. The idea behind the balance is the idea of a carefully weighted scale, and indeed, a situation in which political power between two groups has been placed on a balance is usually the product of many intricate adjustments. True to this image, the Federation has had many wars with the Klingons, Romulans, and Cardassians, but at the time of *The Next Generation* in the twenty-fourth century these wars are all in the past. The present peace is the result of a variety of settlements delineating the borders of the galaxy. Under a balance of power, the opposing parties do not seek extended contact with each other. Neutral zones with the Klingons and Romulans were established by treaty as buffers precisely to prevent contact. By the time we meet the Cardassians in "The Wounded," the balance has already been set and weighted. The aim is to keep things the way they are, no better, no worse. The robust and aggressive James T. Kirk of the original series has been replaced by Jean-Luc Picard, a smaller and older man. Though Picard is a master diplomat, we rarely see him negotiating a new peace (in *The Next Generation* specialized mediators usually perform that function). Picard's job is not to make the peace but to preserve the balance of power. He is often involved in a series of holding actions to keep the various powers of the galaxy in check. One of these is the subject of "Chain of Command."

The episode is divided into two parts, and both parts reveal very different things about how *Star Trek* views the balance of power. The first part of "Chain of Command" sets up a standard scenario of spies, secret weapons, and behind-the-scenes diplomacy. The second part takes us much deeper into the balance of power. Part two shows us the inner workings of the balance as two men, Picard and Gul Madred, confront one another in the recesses of a torture chamber.

The first part of "Chain of Command" is a fairly typical *Star Trek* episode involving espionage and intrigue between the galaxy's great powers. Starfleet Intelligence has found evidence that the Cardassians are developing "metagenic" weapons, biological weapons that release toxins into an atmosphere, toxins designed to seek out and destroy every form of DNA they encounter. Starfleet now believes the Cardassians have been testing a new way of launching metagenic material on Celtris Three, and that is where Starfleet sends the commando team of Picard, Worf, and Crusher in an attempt to destroy the weapons laboratory.

The attempt fails and Picard is captured. Worf and Crusher return to the *Enterprise,* where the new captain, Edward Jellico, is conducting negotiations with the Cardassians. Jellico refuses to admit that Picard was on a mission for the Federation; the Cardassian representative, Gul Lemec, refuses to answer any questions about the installation on Celtris Three. Suspicion and distrust fill the air. This part of the episode effectively conveys the tense reality of a superpower standoff barely held in check by diplomacy. The space opticals seen during the negotiation scenes in "Chain of Command" show the *Enterprise* hovering next to two Galor-class Cardassian warships. The image, repeated again and again in many other episodes dealing with the Romulans and Klingons, is one of suspension, not action. The ships have immense potential power, and the aim of both sides is not to harness it. The great powers of the galaxy face one another across a great divide.

The first part of "Chain of Command" ends with this impasse. If "Chain of Command" had been an ordinary episode of *Star Trek,* it would have simply ended with the discovery and destruction of the metagenic weapon. Lieutenant Geordi La Forge would somehow trace its waves to its source, or Commander William Riker would somehow trick the Cardassians into disclosing its whereabouts. But here there is no metagenic weapon. The Cardassians devised the fiction of the metagenic weapon because they knew the Federation would send Picard, who once conducted extensive tests on theta-band carrier waves when he served on the *Stargazer.* They have set a trap not for the Federation but for Picard himself. Most of the second part of "Chain of Command" shows Picard in an interrogation room, strapped to an interview chair, tortured by a Cardassian inquisitor named Gul Madred. While back on the *Enterprise,* everything is large, invoking the specter of intergalactic war, but in the interrogation room everything is very small and highly personalized.

The torture of Picard is the most graphically violent scene in all of *Star Trek.* It begins with Picard under the influence of a truth serum, answering every question put to him. At first Picard is blindfolded and his hands are manacled. Then he is implanted with a small device capable of producing pain in any part of his body. Then he is stripped naked and hung from a metal rack. Each succeeding scene becomes all the more intense because after a certain point we know that Picard is not being tortured for more information. Under sedation he has already told Gul Madred everything he knows about his mission to Celtris Three. But Madred continues to torture Picard for the sake of torture, almost for the pleasure of it.

In a particularly chilling twist Picard's inquisitor is made out to be a cultured and civilized man. He is an epicure who offers Picard a Cardassian delicacy, boiled taspar egg. Madred shares Picard's interest in archaeology, asking him if he would care to tour the Hebitian burial vaults on Cardassia Prime. Madred is even something of an aesthete. At one point, referring to Picard's experience of incarceration and torture, Madred tells him something even more extraordinary: that he is offering Picard the opportunity for the experience to be—"civilized."

Civilization and barbarity come very close to one another here. Madred is not speaking of civilization to a man over the dinner table; he is speaking to a man twitching with pain. In our own time people have often asked how it was possible for cultured Germans to have run the death camps at Auschwitz, Birkenau, and Buchenwald. Many have wondered how German soldiers could possibly have reconciled the slaughter of the camps with the Bach and Beethoven they played in the barracks, or with the gardens they planted just outside the wire. In "Chain of Command" Madred goes so far as to bring in his daughter to witness the torture of Picard, playing with the little girl and her pet as Picard groans in agony. The juxtaposition is striking. The civilized act of a father playing with his daughter. The barbaric act of one man torturing another. The scene is a reminder that there is irrationality present in even this most rational of universes. The *Star Trek* universe may have improved technically on our own world, feeling the galaxy with food replicators and vastly increasing the speed of travel, but the series constantly reminds us that technical rationality has its limits. This episode is an attempt to see that even in a time of immense technical rationality human beings cannot entirely escape their own irrational urges. There is no reason for Madred to continue the torture of Picard, except to dominate him. The point is not to extract information from Picard but to break him. In the interrogation room of "Chain of Command" the vast concerns of interstellar diplomacy are contracted to the compass of two men, one administering pain, the other experiencing it.

After a certain point, then, Madred aims not at extracting information from Picard but at breaking down his personality. This attempt to win control over his individual identity leads to one of the most remarkable scenes in the series. In the fourth act Madred gestures toward a light fixture on the wall behind him and asks Picard how many lights he sees. There are four lights, and Picard tells Madred that he sees four. "I see five," says Madred, activating the pain device implanted in Picard's chest. Madred continues inflicting pain on Picard, but Picard resists and tells him the truth. "There are four lights," he insists. Facing almost certain death, Picard refuses to deny himself.

What is striking here is that the number of lights in the interrogation room is arbitrary and unrelated to the political situation in the episode. The emphasis of the series is always on the individual. In *Star Trek* all acts are individual acts. The political concerns of "Chain of Command" are completely eclipsed by what Madred is doing to Picard. What we are left with is pain: the pain of hunger, delirium, blinding light. The experience of pain may well be the most isolating experience of human individuality. By the end of "Chain of Command," Picard is naked and screaming but still himself. Jellico and Riker manage to force the Cardassians to return him, but in the last scene of the episode Picard meets with Counselor Deanna Troi in his Ready Room and confesses how close he came to breaking down. He tells her, "I was ready to tell him anything he wanted . . . anything at all. But more than that, I was beginning to *believe* there were five lights." Here as elsewhere, as we shall see in many other episodes, the ultimate nightmare the series has to offer is not the breakdown of political stability in the quadrant but the breakdown of the inner stability of the individual. The political balance of power is not nearly so important as the inner balance of power inside the individual. The two parts of "Chain of Command" set up a clear progression: the superpower confrontation of the first part leads to the personal confrontation of the second. After a certain point we see Picard acting not to preserve the balance of power but to retain his very sanity. The name of his Cardassian adversary mirrors this very struggle, for Madred is a contraction of the words "madness" and "dread," implying the fear of madness that underlies the episode.

But for now the balance of power seems to be working. Picard is returned to the *Enterprise* and things slowly return to normal. The great powers of the galaxy are once again held in check because they are so evenly matched. In "Chain of Command" the threat that one of them may possess the capacity to destroy the other turns out to be completely bogus. The Cardassians may be planning to invade the Federation, but at no point do they contemplate violating the treaty banning the military use of genetically engineered viruses. Far from trying to upset the balance of power, they seem intent on observing it. They buy time by engaging in intricate deceptions. They never break off negotiations. And they pursue clear and limited objectives. In "Chain of Command" the Cardassians plan to invade not the entire Federation but a small sector called Minos Korva. The name of the sector shows how minimal the Cardassian threat actually is. Minos was the king of ancient Crete who built the labyrinth, the legendary maze with no way out. This episode of *Star Trek* ends with the Cardassian invasion fleet near Minos, trapped in a nebula in which their sensors are useless. The implication is that they too are caught in a labyrinth. There is no easy way out of a balance of power in which every action requires an adjusting action of the part of an opponent. If the Cardassian Union sends more ships to the border, so does the Federation. The metaphor of the labyrinth also implicitly compares the experience of the balance of power to the experience of being lost in a maze. In the universe of high diplomacy every action seems to lead in a thousand different directions. "Chain of Command" is full of conferences in which delegates of both sides debate which step to take next. Throughout the episode the Federation and the Cardassian Union really share the same aim: not to upset the balance of power but only to adjust it slightly in their favor.

So we see that the universe of *The Next Generation* is mostly a universe in a state of standoff. At no point in the series do any of the Federation's conventional enemies pose a real threat to its continuing existence. The real threat comes from elsewhere. As in our own world, the real threat to a superpower standoff usually come from within. Societies do not remain in stasis during a long period governed by a balance of power. They must change and adapt to the circumstances of the standoff. A tilt of the balance of power rarely results from a direct attack of one power on the other. The balance tilts because one power can no longer keep it up. As with the Cold War, where the Soviet Union collapsed due to its own internal pressures, a balance of power usually ends due to the internal dissolution of one of the principals. This does not happen to the Federation in *Star Trek* (though it does to the Klingons in the film *Star Trek VI: The Undiscovered Country*), but the series is full of stirrings showing the Federation in a potentially divided state. The program consistently shows the highest levels of the Federation to be in a state of constant turmoil. Anyone at the rank of admiral is generally untrustworthy. In "Descent" Vice Admiral Alynna Nechayev tries to persuade Picard to use a weapon of mass destruction. In "Ensign Ro" Admiral Kennelly conspires to kill a group of displaced Bajorans to placate the Cardassians. In "Conspiracy" at least four different admirals turn out to be spies. When he was designing the original series in the mid-1960s, Gene Roddenberry made the decision that the *Enterprise* should never return to earth, and with good reason. Starfleet Command is a less than ideal organization. The farther away we get from earth, the better it looks.

The danger from within varies from episode to episode. Mostly the danger is seen as coming in isolated and sporadic incidents, as discussed earlier in "The Wounded," where a renegade captain commandeers his ship and starts shooting at the Cardassians. "The Drumhead" offers a more disturbing scenario, for it sees the threat as far more systemic. In this episode yet another admiral forces a confrontation with Picard. Retired Admiral Norah Satie has arrived to investigate the sabotage of the *Enterprise*'s warp drive. She begins to suspect a medical assistant named Simon Tarses. Tarses admits under questioning to being part Vulcan. When she finds out that Tarses has been lying about his ancestry, that he is, in fact, part Romulan, she convenes a formal court of inquiry.

The inquiry is a parody of justice. Satie presumes Tarses's guilt rather than his innocence. She opens the hearing to spectators to put public pressure on Picard to convict. And she cuts off Dr. Crusher when she steps forward to speak of Tarses's good character. During a recess, Picard takes Worf aside and compares this to a "drumhead" trial of five centuries earlier, when military officers would dispense quick summary justice from the podium of an upended drum on the battlefield. When the hearing reconvenes, Picard tells the assembled group that they are hounding an innocent man. Admiral Satie threatens to get rid of Picard if he continues to stand in her way. She goes so far as to say that she is willing to investigate every last person on the ship, starting with him. When Picard tries to defend crewman Tarses, Satie crosses a line. She claims she has evidence that Captain Picard violated the Prime Directive a total of nine times. When Worf tries to defend him, she impugns his abilities as security officer and returns to Picard, whom she accuses of being a traitor to the Federation because he was once a prisoner of the Borg.

Admiral Satie is of course brought down and discredited, but she comes very close to turning a minor incident into a major inquisition. It serves to remind us that the United Federation of Planets often closely resembles the other governments of the galaxy. From the vantage point of the *Enterprise,* the Klingons, Romulans, and Cardassians can often seem to be immersed in the dynamics of *realpolitik,* the theory of politics that whatever is possible is permissible. But as soon as we take a step beyond the *Enterprise,* we find that the rest of the Federation, like most other organizations in history, tends to become so preoccupied with its own preservation that it loses sight of its own purpose. The other cultures in the series are routinely represented as empires acting exclusively in their own self-interest. But the Federation can also act like an empire in its relentless expansion into outer space. Here it is worth recalling that one half of the very title of the series, *Trek,* comes from an Afrikaans word meaning a slow and arduous journey toward a new colony. The situation it evokes, that of nineteenth-century Dutch colonists expanding into an African continent already occupied by a variety of tribes, pushing them off their ancestral lands, and nearly exterminating them, serves to remind us that expansion always comes at a cost. The Dutch, and the British after them, had to abandon their principles to establish an empire in South Africa, as they learned far too late. Under apartheid the rule of law becomes a parody of law. The danger facing the Federation in *Star Trek* is that the exploration of the galaxy will indeed become another "trek" in which the goals and ideals of the Federation will have been abandoned along the way.

If, with the exception of a few minor stirrings such as in "The Drumhead," the balance of power seems to be holding among the major powers of the universe of *The Next Generation,* there is one overriding reason. There is a parity of species in the galaxy; the species belonging to the major powers of the galaxy are really more alike than not. Again we come back to this central premise of *Star Trek:* the essentially human character of the universe. Despite all the nonhuman forms of life in the universe, the most powerful life-forms consistently assume human form. The Klingons and Romulans and Cardassians are all roughly human in stature and appearance. Even the mischievous Q and his friends in the Continuum appear only as humans. So does the Traveler. When the Changelings of the Dominion begin to pose a threat to earth in *Deep Space Nine,* they only do so by assuming human form. No nonhuman form appears beyond the frame of a single episode. This reliance on human form could be seen as anthropocentric, a return to the old belief that human beings are the center of the universe. But in *Star Trek* it is more. Gene Roddenberry created a universe in which species have not developed in complete isolation but are part of a larger web of relationship. The Klingons may have heavy ridged foreheads, the Romulans may have pointy ears, and the Cardassians may have reptilian spines, but they all have four limbs, two front-facing eyes, and a distinct face. This is more than a necessity imposed by makeup men on the studio back lot. *Star Trek* is perfectly capable of summoning monsters when it feels like it; the last chapter of this book will deal with them in their turn. But the fact is that the *Star Trek* universe is a familiar universe full of beings with unfamiliar faces and familiar shapes. Could they all possibly be related?

One of the great speculative moments of the series comes in "The Chase," an episode of *The Next Generation* that examines the origin of its many species with great self-awareness. Professor Richard Galen arrives on the *Enterprise* bearing a gift. He is a famous archaeologist, a former teacher of Picard's who now gives him a terra-cotta figurine, vaguely human in shape. The figurine is a Kurlan naiskos over twelve thousand years old. Its top half separates from its bottom half, revealing a hollow interior filled with a dozen small figurines shaped exactly like the original. Picard explains that "the Kurl believed every individual is a community of individuals . . . each with its own desires, its own way of viewing the world." Not long after Galen leaves the *Enterprise,* his shuttle comes under attack by a Yridian destroyer and he is killed.

The mystery is why someone would go to so much trouble over a professor of archaeology. Dr. Crusher goes over Galen's logs and determines that he had been collecting DNA fragments from planets scattered across the quadrant. The pattern of the DNA reveals it to be over four billion years old. Apparently someone scattered this genetic material into the primordial soup of at least nineteen different planets of the galaxy. The overall DNA pattern appears to contain a message from an old and highly advanced civilization, a message hidden in the fabric of life itself. The completed sequence of DNA triggers a holographic image of a humanoid, dressed in a simple robe, who explains that life evolved on her planet before all others, and that her race scattered this genetic material across the galaxy in hope that they would one day evolve in harmonious form. The messenger's hope that the species of the galaxy would have found common cause in coming to the Vilmoran system turns out to be naive at best and dangerous at worst. They came not because of a disinterested pursuit of knowledge but because they were all jockeying for position in the galactic balance of power.

Picard alone sees the possibilities. In the last scene we again see him contemplating the naiskos. The naiskos, symbol of the one individual full of many desires, is now a symbol of the many progeny derived from the one ancestor. In both cases the many have been derived from the one. There is a sense of symbolic congruence as we see Picard in the final shot, standing at the window in his Ready Room, one man contemplating the vastness of outer space. The hope is that the many species of the galaxy may someday come to appreciate their common origin and see themselves as parts of a greater common whole.

"The Chase" may end on a hopeful note, but looked at more closely, the episode also begins to explain why things are so tense in the *Star Trek* universe. In "The Chase" everyone is related, and though the episode give us some cause for hope, with the Romulan captain recognizing that they may be more alike than not, likeness definitely has its downside. The *Star Trek* universe is full of blood feuds. A blood feud is a feud among close relatives, and it is perhaps the most intractable form of conflict ever known. According to *Star Trek,* an astonishingly high percentage of conflict in the galaxy is blood feud. The Romulans hate the Vulcans because they are related, and in "Unification" they try to invade Vulcan. Klingon violence is always directed most implacably at other Klingons. Threats to the Federation often come from the highest levels of Starfleet Command, especially from its admirals. One of the best episodes of the original series, "Let That Be Your Last Battlefield," shows Kirk caught between two warring species, one with faces half-black and half-white, the other with faces half-white and half-black. In *The Next Generation* the *Enterprise* is forever mediating blood feuds, or ferrying in mediators to do the job for them. The blood feud is first of all a model of political parity in which conflict is permanent but neither side is able to prevail. The blood feud exhibits the ultimate balance of power, and many of the *Enterprise*'s smaller missions reflect in microcosm the larger power structure of a galaxy populated with contending and equally matched species. But most of all the blood feud is a model of likeness in a universe of seemingly dissimilar species. It is very hard for the crew of the *Enterprise* to summon up much antipathy, or even to enter into sustained conflict, with any species too unlike itself. Even the Changeling members of the Dominion must assume human form to cause anxiety on earth. For there to be conflict, there must be likeness. The prevalence of the blood feud is an unexpected testimony to likeness among life-forms in the universe. The fate of likeness remains very much an open question, as in "The Chase," where the discovery of a common ancestor nearly leads to a war between the major powers of the galaxy.

The Federation manages to defeat most of its threats from within, and at least stave off most of its threats from comparable species. But the series does not let the universe rest in a state of comparative stasis. "The Chase" shows that the species of the galaxy have evolved to a certain point. But what if human evolution were to have taken a slightly different direction? Evolution, after all, presupposes change: the species of today may not be the species of tomorrow; the balance of species is as easily upset as the balance of power. In "The Chase" the idea of a common ancestor giving birth to a variety of species also carries with it the idea that some of those species may not survive forever. When Charles Darwin wrote *Origin of Species,* he tried to trace the many modifications by which one species supplants another as it evolves into a higher form. The species in *Star Trek* are all at a rough stage of parity in their evolutionary development, but according to Darwin, a question always remains. What if another humanoid species were to take a great evolutionary step forward and supersede all the others? Darwin's book is full of examples of species that did not make it to the modern world, species that were wiped out by more powerful species that happened to have evolved alongside them. "The Chase" views all the humanoid species in the galaxy as related and roughly equal, but what if, as Darwin assumes, a new and advanced mutation were to appear on the scene? A new kind of human species with a completely superior physical, social, and technical organization? A species as superior to us as we were to *Mesopithecus*? What would become of the balance of power in the galaxy? What, then, would become of the Prime Directive?

3

This species is the Borg. In many ways the Borg are the classic space invaders of science fiction. They come from out of nowhere. They are unstoppable, possessing a superior technology with a social organization to match. They do not care about their losses. They are something like pure invaders and they pose the only genuine threat to the Federation ever seen in all the four series and eight movies. But they are more than mere invaders. They do not pose a political or military threat the way the Klingons, Romulans, or Cardassians sometimes do. They pose a fundamental threat to the continued existence, to the very being, of the human species itself. They are part human and part machine, and the way they work is by mutilation, by taking humans and transforming them into aggregates of flesh and circuitry. They do not seek to establish an empire in the usual sense of a conqueror ruling over subject peoples. They seek to transform all species into Borg, destroying their will to resist by seeking out and destroying their identities as individuals, one by one.

Among species, the Borg are in a class of their own. The rest of the species in the *Star Trek* universe all use machines as tools. The Borg are a race fully integrated with machines. Borg is short for "cyborg," meaning a biologically engineered cybernetic organism. Back in the 1940s the mathematician Norbert Wiener coined the word "cybernetics" to describe the science of integrating human and mechanical control systems. *Star Trek* is full of mechanical devices who manage to achieve a kind of life, such as the exocomps in "The Quality of Life" or Lieutenant Commander Data. But Data is not actually a cybernetic organism. A cybernetic organism is a fully integrated mixture of man and machine. In *Star Trek* as in our own world there remains a great divide between man and machine. Most of the technologies of a starship are fully external to the human body. Its warp engines provide transportation, its phaser banks provide defense, its sensors provide information. The series sets itself apart from most science fiction in that it generally observes the divide between man and machine, with the exception of a few prosthetic devices meant to compensate for a disability, such as Geordi's visor and Picard's artificial heart. There is nothing in the series like Luke Skywalker's prosthetic hand in *Star Wars* or Johnny's brain diodes in *Johnny Mnemonic*. There are no episodes in which Data manages to connect himself to living tissue. Data is generally able to interface with almost any kind of machine, but he is not, in Wiener's definition, a cybernetic organism. He is a machine among men. Throughout the series the great divide between man and machine remains fully intact.

This is why the Borg are such a brilliant addition to the *Star Trek* universe. They are a race based on a kind of technical fusion of man and machine that *Star Trek* maintains almost as a taboo. The world of the Federation may be a very advanced world, but it is not a cybernetic world. At its most fundamental *Star Trek* offers an appealing vision of a future because it offers a vision of a human race that has managed to preserve most of its humanity. Again and again Kirk and Picard give speeches expostulating on the importance of humanity; I would argue that the series advances its vision of humanity by keeping humans human, that is, partly by scrupulously observing this divide between man and machine. None of the other major races in the galaxy, the Klingons or the Romulans or the Cardassians, attempt to violate the integrity of the human body. They all use technology as servants (our word "servomechanism" clearly indicates this slavery of machines), restricting their use for the most part to tools. Things put *inside* the human body, such as implants and parasites, are generally shown in the series to be threats that need to be extracted or eradicated as quickly as possible. The human body must be maintained integral. More often than not, mechanical implants are used as forms of mind control (as in "The Mind's Eye," where Geordi's visor implants are recalibrated by Romulans to control his thoughts) or as forms of torture (as in "Chain of Command," where an implant is used to produce pain in Picard). As if to underscore this need to preserve the integrity of human bodily processes, *The Next Generation* goes so far as to put children on the *Enterprise,* and to devote several episodes to the pregnancy of Starfleet botanist Keiko O'Brien. The twenty-fourth century offers us a vision of a humane society precisely, it seems, because it has maintained the dividing line between man and machine.

The Borg first disrupt this essentially humane universe in an episode called "Q Who?" Disguised as a crewman, Q has transported Picard in a shuttle to an unexplored region of the galaxy inhabited by a species called the Borg. Q has come in order to deliver a warning to Picard: "The Klingons, the Romulans, are nothing compared to what's waiting." Q offers himself as a guide to the wonders and terrors that lie ahead, but Picard turns him down flat. Miffed, Q returns him to the *Enterprise* and strikes the *Enterprise* with a great surge of energy, propelling the ship seven thousand light-years away. The *Enterprise* is now in Borg territory, brought there, Q explains, "to give you a taste of your future."

The role of Q in introducing the Borg deserves further explanation before we go on. Q is essentially a comic character, an omnipotent being with a sense of humor. He frequently exasperates the crew of the *Enterprise,* particularly Picard, but despite his tricks he almost always acts as the protector of Starfleet. Q blends comedy with the essence of a supreme being. That he is so playful and mischievous gives us a hint that the *Star Trek* universe is more comic than tragic, and that the outcome will tend to favor the continuing existence of humanity. Some science fictions, like Isaac Asimov's *Foundation* series and Frank Herbert's *Dune* series, offer essentially tragic visions emphasizing the death of the hero, the demise of civilization, and the futility of all action. Others, like *Star Trek,* offer essentially comic visions emphasizing the triumph of the hero, the flourishing of civilization, and the importance of all action. *Star Trek* certainly has elements of tragedy about it—Picard, after all, is an amateur archaeologist specializing in dead civilizations—but he is the captain of a starship traveling around an essentially comic universe in which the most powerful beings in the universe (Q is one, the Traveler is another) display an amused and sympathetic interest in the fate of humanity. In the Borg saga Q is there to let us know that somewhere, somehow, all is right with the universe, that even in outer space there is a supreme being with a sense of divine comedy. Though Q can often seem to be an enemy of the Federation, he is actually a crucial component of *Star Trek's* comic vision of the universe. He is a reminder that the crew of the *Enterprise* is destined to triumph, that in the end all will be right with the universe, though there might be some adversity along the way.

So when we see Q introducing the Borg to the crew of the *Enterprise,* we know that all will be well. But Q of course disappears to let them find their own destiny, one step at a time. After he snaps his fingers, the *Enterprise* finds itself in a remote and unexplored region of the galaxy. The sensors soon detect a strange ship, shaped like a box. Suddenly a Borg scout beams aboard. The Borg has a metal device implanted in his head. One arm is artificial with a tool instead of a hand. One eye is an enhanced prosthetic device. The Borg steps up to one of the companels and attaches the apparatus on his arm to the computer. He is followed by another, who drains the computer of information about the *Enterprise*. Before Picard can figure anything out, the Borg hail them. A generalized Borg voice, carefully calibrated to sound like an overlay of a thousand voices, tells them, "We have analyzed your defensive capabilities as being unable to withstand us." Picard and his staff now begin to realize that they are dealing not with an individual mind, but with the collective minds of all the Borg, fused in one physio-technological entity, the square black Borg ship.

The square is a particularly appropriate shape for the Borg ship. A square is a geometric figure with four sides of equal length and four right angles. Everything in a square is the product of equal factors. "Square" also has a second meaning as a number raised to the second power. The Borg collective displays both elements of the square in a frightening way: it represents a collective composed of equal parts, containing no repeated dimensions, and it suggests the possibility of the rapid linear reproduction of those parts by an endless multiplying to the second power. The duality of the square is a terrifying figure for the double threat posed by the Borg. For not only are the Borg a collective, threatening what may be the most sacred value of the *Star Trek* universe, the integrity of the human individual, but the Borg threaten to multiply and fill the universe with a single collective mind that will spell the end of human individuality. In the figure of the square the crew of the *Enterprise* confronts a compressed image the Borg pose to the continued existence of humanity itself. The fear is that they may be the next step up the evolutionary ladder, a race of beings better adapted to life in outer space. The square ship is again a pure image of the immense practicality of the Borg, as well as a reminder that they have evolved into a society which all form follows function, for whereas all the other starships seen in the series are aerodynamic, relics of the days of air travel on individual planets, only the Borg have discovered that starships in space do not have to be stream-lined. They can be more efficient by being square.

The crew members of the *Enterprise* make further discoveries about the Borg when they board the square ship after an exchange of fire. There are hundreds, perhaps thousands, of Borg around them, mounted in individual slots, hooked up to the ship. They also discover a nursery, full of infants in various stages of cybernetic fusion with machines. Via subspace Riker tells Picard that the Borg seem to be born biologically, then implanted with technological elements—and their species seems to have no females. Riker is right; there are no female Borg. The species is exclusively male. This is one of the most chilling moments in the Borg trilogy, and with good reason. Here men have learned to reproduce without women. In Mary Shelley's old story of Dr. Frankenstein, one man managed to create another man without a woman being involved, and the result was a monster. Like Frankenstein's monster, mon-sters in science fiction tend to be beings that have bypassed the ordinary channels of sexual reproduction. Throughout *Star Trek* no species displaying the traits of gender is ever treated as monstrous. Where there is distinct gender, there is no monstrosity.

Star Trek has always been very protective of the system of two distinct genders. From the beginning it was among the first science fiction programs to show men and women working together in space. *The Next Generation* goes so far as to put families on a starship. No matter what the species, *Star Trek* always treats the situation of a mother protecting her young very sympathetically, devoting a number of episodes to showing the *Enterprise* helping the infant along ("The Devil in the Dark" in the original series, "Junior" in *The Next Generation*). The series even has an episode, "The Outcast," showing people on an androgenous planet that has criminalized gender. Citizens with male or female tendencies are brainwashed into androgyny. The need to maintain gender is so strong that Picard knowingly allows Riker and Worf to violate the Prime Directive by undertaking a rescue mission after they have been asked to leave the planet. In "Q Who?" it is appropriate that Will Riker, the most sexually active member of the crew, makes the discovery of the Borg nursery. In episode after episode he is attracted to females of many different species. Like James T. Kirk before him, the sexually effusive Riker represents the possibilities for human reproduction in outer space. The contrast between Riker and the Borg could not be greater. Riker shows human drives unaffected by interstellar travel. The Borg show that it is possible to begin life as a human being and end it as a cybernetic organism.

"Q Who?" ends with the *Enterprise* managing to evade the grip of the Borg, but only barely. Q reappears and taunts Picard for his previous smugness and arrogance, asking him, "Do you still profess to be prepared for what awaits you [in space]?" Q is right. In a way the Federation is arrogant. The crew of the *Enterprise* is a little too perfect, a little too supremely confident in its own manifest destiny to explore the final frontier. Q has come to cut human beings and their allies down to size, and as we have seen, he has good reason to do so. So far the *Star Trek* universe has been full of less developed cultures, for whose benefit the Prime Directive was fashioned, and equal cultures, held in check by the balance of power. In all of the series the Borg are the first culture to be placed in a superior position. In this episode Q comes to the *Enterprise* like a god coming to earth to warn humanity that it has overreached its bounds. Though Q winds up returning the *Enterprise* to Federation space with a wave of his wrist, the warning is effective. The possibility not of gradual human development but of sudden human extinction now enters the series.

The complacency sometimes seen in the series, Starfleet's serene confidence in humanity's mission to explore the galaxy, is further shattered in the second segment of the Borg trilogy, a two-part episode called "The Best of Both Worlds." In "Q Who?" Q intervenes before we can find out what the Borg will do to human beings once they defeat them. Q does not play a role in the rest of the Borg trilogy, but overtones of divine guidance and goodwill persist. The distress call at the beginning of "The Best of Both Worlds" comes from a colony called New Providence, implying once again that it is for the general good of humanity that it confront the Borg. But in this episode the confrontation takes a frightening new twist. From the previous incident Starfleet knows that the Borg are immensely powerful cybernetic species. But what do the Borg want? What motivates them?

The answer to these questions occupies the entire episode, one of the most remarkable in the series. When the *Enterprise* answers the call at New Providence, the crew find that there is nothing left of the colony. Soon they are confronted by a Borg who demands that Picard transport himself aboard their vessel. This moment is very powerful. The Borg are, after all, a collective species with no distinct individuals, and here all they want is Picard. Fighting erupts and the *Enterprise* suffers an outer hull breach almost immediately. A group of Borg penetrate the shields and board the *Enterprise*. On the bridge they look around for a moment, identify Picard, move toward him, and grab him. A second later he dematerializes in a transporter beam.

Picard finds himself in the cavernous interior of the Borg ship. Picard tells the Borg he will resist them with the last ounce of his strength, but the Borg again speak to him with a thousand synchronized voices, saying that it is futile to resist and that his culture will be adapted to service theirs. Characteristically, Picard continues to ask them not only what they are doing but why they are doing it. The Borg finally give a single deafening answer to Picard's repeated questions: "We wish to improve ourselves."

This statement may seem incredible at first sight, but looked at more closely, it makes complete sense. The Borg are the ultimate culture of self-improvement. They show that every improvement to a culture comes at a cost. To increase and multiply, any culture must consume things and dominate people. There are many examples of this process in our own history, where the expansion of one culture generally requires the contraction of another. Imperial expansion creates subject peoples. New technologies require raw materials and create waste. Even culture itself is generally developed for the few rather than for the many. The Borg are a culture of self-improvement taken to its logical conclusion. To improve themselves, they are willing to consume anything and everything in their way. But each time the Borg improve themselves, it is at the direct expense of another culture whose life and technology they have consumed in their continuing quest for betterment. The implication here is that the Borg might not be able to survive without cultures to consume. Cultures are like food to them, and they stalk them like a predator seeking prey. Despite their perfectly functional culture, they do not occupy a self-contained universe. They actually *need* other species, if only to consume them. Their quest for collective self-improvement is thus actually a kind of dependency, for collective cultures like the Borg have to consume individuals in order to remain collective.

So they have seized Picard to use his knowledge of the Federation against his own people. When an away team boards the Borg ship, they find that Picard has been turned into a Borg. Half his face is gone, replaced with black tubular implants. The away team is unable to extract him from the Borg ship and beams back to the *Enterprise* just in time to see Picard come on the viewscreen. Picard stuns them when he says: "I am Locutus of Borg. From this time forward, you will service . . . *us.*"

The image of Picard remade into a Borg has become one of the most famous images of the series, and for good reason. It represents the confrontation of the most deeply rooted values of the *Star Trek* universe, the values of human freedom and self-determination, with something like their pure opposite. The *Star Trek* universe is a bit like the universe of the novels of Charles Dickens, full of distinct and memorable characters who move through complex and confusing plots. It is often hard to remember, let alone to reconstruct, the details of any given *Star Trek* plot, but the glue that holds it all together is always the single solitary individual. Individuality persists throughout every surprise the universe can throw at the *Enterprise,* and the interest the series often holds for us derives from specific character traits we learn to expect again and again: Picard's request to the replicator for "Tea, Earl Grey, hot," Riker's trombone playing, Worf's Klingon calisthenics, Data's interest in Sir Arthur Conan Doyle. Similarly, the relationships forged between individuals, the friendships of Data and Geordi, Worf and Riker, Picard and Crusher, form the basis of action and can often alter the course of a story. But in the Borg world there is no individuality. Picard is stripped of his identity in order to serve as a spokesman for the Borg. The image of Picard remade as a Borg is like an icon of the series confronting its own deepest fears, the destruction of the individual by the technological society.

The second part of "The Best of Both Worlds" comes as close to interstellar Armageddon as any episode in the series. The Borg ship continues its unstoppable course toward earth. Picard has become fully Borg, feeding his knowledge and experience as Jean-Luc Picard into the collective, which the Borg use to rout the Starfleet armada just short of earth. We do not actually see the battle, but the optical showing its aftermath is one of the most haunting of the series, panning over the wreckage of the armada, a cemetery of ships.

The *Enterprise* now must face the Borg alone. Riker decides not to attack the Borg ship, but to board it and take back Picard. A small away team led by Worf beams aboard the Borg ship and abducts Locutus. The crew of the *Enterprise* disassembles the array of prostheses the Borg have attached to Picard. Only when Picard starts to recover his human identity does the Borg ship slow its approach to earth and turn to intercept the *Enterprise*. Picard revives enough to give them a clue: a single word, "sleep." Data correctly interprets this as a suggestion to plant a command in the Borg collective consciousness. Working through Picard, he misdirects them to believe that it is time to regenerate. In effect he puts them all to sleep. The Borg attack simply ends and the Borg withdraw from our solar system.

"The Best of Both Worlds" thus ends very provisionally. The Borg threat still exists and Starfleet must rebuild and prepare for it. If anything, the Borg have demonstrated their complete technological superiority. One Borg ship has managed to destroy half of Starfleet: we can only imagine what an armada of such ships would do to earth. Picard himself has to begin a long road to recovery, a recovery that will take another full episode to detail ("Family"). The last scenes of this episode successfully convey Picard's exhaustion; this, more than any of his other experiences on board the *Enterprise,* has left him a changed man. And yet the clear implication of the title of the episode, "The Best of Both Worlds," is that this change is for the better. It may not be readily evident at this moment, but Picard now understands the Borg. As a prisoner of the Borg, he was forced to use his knowledge of Starfleet against his own people. But now, returning home, the implication is that he will be able to take the sum and substance of what he learned among the Borg and use it not for purposes of revenge but for the general good, for the best of both worlds.

He does so in the concluding episode in the Borg trilogy, "I, Borg." Like a lot of the very best episodes of *Star Trek,* it depends not only on events taking place in this particular episode but on knowledge built up over a preceding series of episodes. The *Enterprise* picks up a distress call coming from a small moon orbiting a planet. They locate the crash site of a ship and find one badly wounded survivor. He is a Borg. Picard consents to have the wounded Borg beamed up. Geordi begins work on an invasive programming sequence, a computer virus to be carried back to the collective by this Borg, infecting the collective and disabling their neural network in one stroke.

Geordi asks the Borg if he has a name. The Borg says, "Third, of five," meaning he was the third of five crew members on his small ship. The Borg does not understand that he has the beginnings of a personality; that he is shy, slight, and innocent; that Geordi is trying to befriend him.

Geordi is the perfect choice of a human to befriend the Borg. He has an almost inbred affinity with machines. Not only does he wear the only visible prosthesis in the series, his visor, but his very name,

La Forge, links him to one of the oldest traditions of human contact with machines, the blacksmith's forge. In Western tradition, the forge traditionally has a double meaning. The blacksmith forges tools and household implements of general use to humanity, but the blacksmith also forges weapons that allow human beings to kill one another. The image of the blacksmith can be either peaceful or violent, and this is the tension that persists throughout Geordi's relationship with the Borg survivor. As an individual, this Borg seems to be harmless enough, but as a member of his collective, he is more menacing than any species encountered in the *Star Trek* universe. But as the episode proceeds, the captured Borg takes on an identity as something other than a member of the general Borg collective.

The naming of the Borg is the key scene in the episode. After running a few tests, Geordi again asks the Borg for his name. This time, though, they speak as friends rather than captors, introducing themselves first. Then Geordi has a thought. "That's it. Hugh. What do you think?" The Borg hesitates, then, in an astonishing leap, he gets it. He says, "We are Hugh." This leap from "you" to "Hugh," so close in sound, is a remarkable testimony to the closeness of individuality and identity. "You" is our generic term for another individual. "Hugh" is the name of a person. The implication is that any "you," that is, any distinct individual, has behind him a name, even if only a potential name. Geordi was perfectly ready to regard "Three, of five" as a valid name, but now he gives the Borg a name that is at once concrete and abstract. The name is a perfect bridge between the abstractness of "you" and the concreteness of "Hugh." It has a residue of collective identity and yet is fully human and fully specific. A crucial transition has here been made, from abstract to concrete, from collective to individual, from alien to almost human.

Now that the Borg has a name, the crew of the *Enterprise* can no longer look on him as a monster. Geordi in particular begins to have doubts about sending back Hugh as a walking bomb to destroy the others in the collective. By now a Borg ship is approaching to investigate the crash, and Picard must make up his mind quickly. Picard confronts the Borg and is amazed to discover that Hugh now uses "I" instead of "we." After a real internal struggle, Picard decides that his ideals of freedom and self-determination should apply equally to the Borg. They return him to the planet, where he is reconnected with the Borg arriving from the rescue ship. But just as they are about to beam up, Hugh's eyes meet those of Geordi, who is observing from a safe distance. Those eyes still have about them the unmistakable mark of individuality.

The Borg appear in a number of other episodes, but the struggle against them is fully played out in this clear trilogy of episodes: "Q Who?", "The Best of Both Worlds," and "I, Borg." By the end of "I, Borg," it is clear that the completely collective society the Borg represent is a failure. The Borg are not defeated by a vast alliance or by a secret weapon. The Borg are brought down by a single solitary individual, or more generally, by the segregation of minds brought on by the beginnings of individual consciousness. We get a premonition of this when Picard manages to retain something of his identity after his absorption into the Borg. When he comes on the viewscreen, startling the bridge crew with his whitened skin, pink eyes, and tubular implants, he nevertheless tells them, "I am Locutus of Borg." In other words, despite his absorption, Picard is the only member of the Borg collective who has a name. Even more striking, the Borg are the ones who named him. Somewhere in their collective consciousness they have retained the capacity to identify specific individuals. Locutus comes from the Latin verb *allocutus,* which means "to address." Picard is here named very generally, by his function, "the one who addresses." Nevertheless, in our own history, this naming by function is the very origin of naming. Names, particularly common last names, are often initially derived from specific functions. A Sawyer is one who saws wood; a Cooper is one who makes barrels; a Taylor is one who sews clothes. In the Borg trilogy the Federation may not have been fully responsible for causing an outbreak of individuality among the Borg. They already possessed the capacity to give Picard a last name, Locutus. Indeed they clearly possess the ability to want to seize a specific individual in the first place. All they needed to be taught was how to give a first name, and the giving of the first name, Hugh Borg, was of course the subject of the third part of the Borg trilogy, "I, Borg."

The Borg trilogy would have been the best extended story *Star Trek* ever told had it stopped there. Unfortunately, the Borg appear in a number of later episodes in which the tragic threat posed by the Borg inadvertently becomes the stuff of low comedy. In "Descent" Data's evil brother commandeers a group of Borg, newly confused by their own nascent identities, who end up stumbling across the screen like a bunch of wind-up toys. But this lack of restraint in pushing every story toward comedy should hardly come as a surprise. As I explained earlier, *Star Trek* runs an essentially comic universe, and the clear tendency of every episode is toward comedy, not tragedy. Comedy always frames tragedy in *Star Trek:* this is why "Q Who?" begins with a long and fairly irrelevant comic scene in which a young ensign spills coffee all over Captain Picard. Almost every episode in the series ends on an upbeat comic note, showing one of the characters teasing another about some predictable foible, such as Spock's logic or Picard's formality. Though some of this comedy verges on formulaic gags, it actually performs an important function within the *Star Trek* universe. The typical episode of *Star Trek* ends with laughter. This laughter may be corny and sometimes downright stupid, but it goes a long way toward explaining why *Star Trek* is the most popular of all science fictions. Science fiction is generally a glum genre full of wars, invasions, and other traumas in which contact leads to conflict and annihilation. *Star Trek* is the only science fiction to have successfully created a comic universe in which contact leads to conflict, resolution, peace, and laughter.

4

So we see that the destiny of the Federation is not exactly manifest. The three scenarios of alien contact examined here propose three radically different versions of Federation history. In "Who Watches the Watchers?" the Federation is placed in a distinctly superior position. In "Chain of Command" the Federation faces an equal opponent. In the Borg trilogy the Federation faces annihilation. These are not just different episodes in a continuing series of episodes. They represent a distinct view of history not as a single fate or destiny but as an endless series of possibilities. The Cardassians could very well succeed in one of their attempts to infiltrate the Federation, or the Borg could return and assimilate all of humanity into its collective. The Klingons may or may not choose to remain Federation allies. At every turn the series is full of alternate futures and alternate pasts. No event in the series is final or fated, not even death. The only death of a major character in the series, the death of Tasha Yar, is presented as a senseless and arbitrary act. She dies as the result of a monster's whim, forcing the other characters to meditate on the meaning of an accidental death. Even when confronted with the basic issues of life and death, *Star Trek* offers a sense of historical time as open and unfixed.

This idea that there is no set trajectory to history is all the more striking when placed in the context of most science fiction. Seen in broad outline, a lot of science fiction is not so far removed from astrology. Astrology, or the belief that the stars influence the course of human events, is perhaps the oldest of science fictions, and most modern science fiction preserves something of the original belief of astrology that there is a determining force behind human events. *Star Trek* differs vastly from the fantasies of most other science fiction in removing a deterministic structure from most of its stories. In the *Star Wars* movies Luke Skywalker is driven to act out his destiny as a Jedi knight. In Asimov's *Foundation* series the predictions of a single man dictate the fate of the galaxy. In Herbert's *Dune* series a body of sacred writings predicts the arrival of a messiah. The Federation inhabits a very different kind of universe. Nothing has to happen the way it does. Though, as we will see in the fourth chapter, *Star Trek* preserves certain other elements of religion, *Star Trek* takes the astrology out of the stars.

This sense of history as radically unfinished is most often explored through the device of parallel universes. Again and again *Star Trek* uses the device of different dimensions to show the contingency of historical events. What if Captain Picard were to have died as a captive of the Borg? What if Lieutenant La Forge were to die of plasma burns after an accident in engineering? What if Will Riker were captain of the *Enterprise*? These are all contingencies Lieutenant Worf encounters in an episode called "Parallels."

The episode begins with Worf returning from winning a Bat'leth sword competition on Forcas Three. Working at his station on the bridge, Worf is struck by a wave of dizziness. He rubs his forehead and closes his eyes. When he opens them, Data and Geordi are both standing at the opposite end of the room. In the fraction of a second everyone on the bridge has changed positions.

The next few scenes show Worf observing many other transformations. Relieved from duty on the bridge, he checks his personal logs. In this frame of reference his shuttle broke down and he never made it to the Bat'leth tournament on Forcas Three. The dizzy spells continue, and the parallel universes grow less and less familiar. There is a degradation of familiarity from scene to scene. The episode begins with minor transformations, such as the movement of objects, and ends with larger transformations, such as different relationships and different histories. By the third act, Data's eyes are no longer gold but blue and human-looking. By the fourth act, Worf is married to Troi. By the fifth act, Riker has become the captain of the *Enterprise.*

It turns out that his shuttlecraft passed through a quantum fissure in the space-time continuum. The fissure is the opening to many different realities, and by entering it Worf began a series of shifts into other realities. Data explains the quantum physics theory that *all* possible outcomes of any event *do* happen in alternate quantum realities. The fissure is a very small speck, and Wesley Crusher has the idea of scanning the fissure using a subspace pulse. But after an attack from a Bajoran ship (in this particular reality, the Bajorans have overthrown the Cardassian empire), the pulse surges and the quantum fissure begins to destabilize. One *Enterprise* appears on the viewscreen, then another, then another. Soon there are thousands. Shock sets in as the crew realizes that, in Data's words, "The barriers between quantum realities are breaking down. Other realities are emerging into our own."

The crew manages to close the fissure, but before they do, a visual near the end of "Parallels" gives us a remarkable vision of historical multiplicity as we see hundreds of possible *Enterprises* stretching off into the distance. Wesley informs the bridge that he is receiving 285,000 hails from other ships. Each of them offers a plausible variation on Federation history. At one point the image of Riker comes on the viewscreen. He looks haggard and terrified. The ship is full of smoke; emergency lights flash in the background. He says urgently, "You don't know what it's like in our universe. The Federation is gone—the Borg are everywhere. Please, you've got to help us!" This could have been the outcome of "The Best of Both Worlds." In that episode the crew of the *Enterprise* managed to avert a cataclysm, but here it returns to haunt them as one possible past leading to one possible future.

This image of the terrified Riker has become one of the most widely reproduced stills from the series, and for good reason. The terrified Riker shows what might have happened, and might happen still. *Star Trek* works from a truly sophisticated sense of history, for the series recognizes that the past is never past. All the irresolution of the past, all its hopes and dreams and failed possibilities, survives on into the present. Even after an event has happened, the event is anything but resolved. It continues to cast its shadow onto the possible futures. Actions in *Star Trek* are never complete, because what could have happened persists. Episodes of *Star Trek* often end in a disturbing moment of irresolution in which the outcome of the episode begins to seem uncertain. In "Conspiracy" Picard and his crew kill a parasite that has infiltrated the highest levels of Starfleet Command. But in the last beat of the episode we hear the sound of a homing beacon sent out by the parasite just before its death. The pulsing of the beacon undermines the certainty of any outcome. For now the parasites are dead. But history might have been different, and it still might be.

The device of parallel universes is offered without much explanation or science to back it up. The most we hear is talk of a "quantum flux." The parallel universe functions as something like a literary device in which the important thing is not the plausibility of the movement but the proliferation of widely divergent scenes. The device of parallel universes is intended to disclose alternate realities based on a fairly stable aggregate of historical circumstances. Here it is worth noting that these different dimensions are not completely alien worlds. A parallel universe is not a completely different universe, but a slightly different variation on our own. Certain things seem to remain stable in parallel universes. The design of the *Enterprise* remains the same in "Parallels," but in other parallel universe episodes, such as "Yesterday's Enterprise," the design of the ship and uniforms is quite different. Significantly, the one constant in these 285,000 alternate universes of "Parallels" is the constant of human character and identity. Though some may live and others may die, the crew members themselves remain the same as we move from dimension to dimension. Parallel universes do not seem to affect personality. Even though disoriented, Worf remains in character, as do the other members of the crew. The historical circumstances vary from dimension to dimension, but the identity of each character remains integral and whole. There may always be an element of arbitrariness to history, but come what may, it does not threaten the integrity of human character.

This continuity of character amid incredible flux has the effect of downplaying the importance of historical circumstance in *Star Trek*. Historical forces remains largely external to character in *Star Trek*. Again and again the real threats to the Federation are cast not as threats to the integrity of Federation territory but as threats to the integrity of human identity. The reason the Borg are so much more threatening than any other enemy is that they threaten not defeat but disindividuation. The breakdown of the human individual is the greatest nightmare *Star Trek* has to offer, and this is unlikely to happen through a shift in mere historical circumstances. Though we have seen that the series is sensitive to the vicissitudes of history,

Star Trek is not primarily interested in the historical world. The vast epic sweep of history seen in so much other science fiction plays only a small role in the series. The *Enterprise* is, after all, just one ship in a fleet of hundreds of ships. If *Star Trek* is a lot more than a big war movie in outer space, the reason ultimately has to do with its focus on character and identity rather than exploration and empire. The first series has eight major characters. *The Next Generation* has ten. The series begins where many other science fictions begin, with the exploration of deep space. But its exploration of the deepest spaces of human identity is what takes it even farther into the unknown.

Chapter Two

CHARACTER
and
IDENTITY

Today the central experience of space exploration is the experience of solitude. Our space vessels go to empty places where our astronauts are alone in space. The film *Apollo 13* very accurately conveys the sense of isolation in space as the capsule starts spinning out of control on its way to the moon. A frail lifeline joins the capsule to earth, a lifeline easily frayed and severed. Take a human being away from the autonomous life-support system of a spaceship and you are left with a solitary human being unsure of his place in the universe. Human beings are social creatures, and as shown in the previous chapter, *Star Trek* has created a very social universe. But the best episodes of the series are not ensemble pieces. The typical

Star Trek episode isolates one character from the rest of the crew and focuses on the personal dilemmas the character faces. Despite the incredible vastness of space, the universe turns out to be a very personal place. The fate of cultures and peoples routinely rests on individual actions. In most science fiction the gods look after human beings, as they do in the *Star Wars* films, where the Force guides the actions of the human beings fighting the Evil Empire. *Star Trek* may be the only science fiction in which an individual human being actually saves the life of a god (when Picard saves the life of "Q" in "Déjà Q"). The universe of *Star Trek* is a universe in which individual action matters far more than divine or collective action. In this series the solitary hero is very much the hero confronting the dynamics of his own solitude.

In *Star Trek* space itself may no longer be a solitary place, but the experience of solitude remains very important to the series. The farther the *Enterprise* strays from earth, the more each individual becomes an island of humanity in a far and desolate place. Away from the *Enterprise* the humanity of each character comes into even more searching question. One of the most common plots running through the series involves separating a crew member from the *Enterprise*. A shuttle crashes in "Liasons." A transporter accident leaves Riker stranded on a planet in "Second Chances." Picard dies and awakens in the afterlife in "Tapestry." Survival in the physical sense is rarely at issue. What is at issue are some of the most fundamental questions about human identity. What does it mean to be human? In what consists the integrity of the human personality? What are the rights of the individual? In these stories the "science" of science fiction drops away and we are left with the ordinary subject of most stories, the development of a single character.

These fundamentally psychological questions may seem far from the universes of most science fiction. Very few science fiction novels give us much of a sense of the inner lives of characters. Good and evil are often strongly delineated, as in the *Star Wars* movies. Ambivalence, doubt, hesitation, and remorse are rarely represented. This tendency toward a mythical construction of reality will be examined in the next chapter; for now suffice it to say that this tendency toward myth often precludes any examination of the inner life of any given character. What we get instead are large actions on an epic scale. The fate of the universe may often hinge on the actions of a single character, but the story allows little or no time for exploring the inner being of its central character. When Martians invade earth in *The War of the Worlds,* there is no time to examine the vicissitudes of character. There is a war to be fought, and questions of character and identity are often placed in suspension for the duration of the narrative. Indeed one of the reasons science fiction has remained a marginal form is that the genre gives its writers license to pursue its large themes at the expense of character. The characters from a novel by Isaac Asimov do not stay with us like the characters in a novel by Charles Dickens or Joseph Conrad. They have an almost expository nature, a nature seen quite clearly in Asimov's *Foundation* novels, where human beings are expected to act in accordance with the predictions of statistics. Much science fiction excels at stripping human beings of their free will, making them into the puppets of large universal forces like planned societies (in the *Foundation* series), systems of religious prophecy (in the *Dune* series), or social codes of conduct (in Doris Lessing's *Shikasta*).

Science fiction did not begin with such a broad sweep. Most critics now agree that Mary Shelley's novel *Frankenstein* (1818) is the first work of science fiction. Given what we have seen the genre develop into, what we should expect in this novel is a large-scale plot of invasion, migration, war, and diaspora. A novel of interplanetary intrigue. A novel in which good and evil square off in a final battle for the soul of the universe. But nothing could be farther from the world of *Frankenstein*. Shelley's novel tells the story of an isolated and highly introspective doctor, Victor Frankenstein. Frankenstein is a marginal man, a medical school dropout. He is the first mad scientist, and the assumption throughout the novel is that the kind of science he is practicing is illegitimate. Science fiction begins here with a basic suspicion of science, not a celebration of science. In fact, the "science" in the novel never fully comes clear. We never really know according to what theory Frankenstein assembles his monster, because Shelley is not at all interested in scientific theories. What is remarkable is that the first work of science fiction is largely a detailed study of the formation of character. In literary history this kind of study is called the *Bildungsroman,* or the novel about growing up. Very few subsequent works of science fiction preserve this interest, though, as we shall see, *The Next Generation* returns to the origins of the genre when it includes as a member of the crew a young boy, Wesley Crusher, and runs him through the major trials of adolescence.

The other remarkable feature of *Frankenstein* is its focus not on the doctor but on the monster. The hero of this novel about a monster turns out to be the monster himself. The 1931 Boris Karloff movie treatment of the monster as a stammering, stupid being does not do justice to the novel. At the beginning of the novel Victor Frankenstein expels the monster from his home, forcing him to live in a desolate area of the Alps. While concealing himself in the mountains, the monster begins to observe the movements of a simple peasant family. He teaches himself how to speak and how to read, and learns a strict moral code by studying the manners of the peasant family. He educates himself, and by the time he tells his story to the novel's initial narrator, Robert Walton, he is modest and well spoken. The genius of the novel is that the monster is the most sensitive character in it. Most of the novel is taken up with the monster's account of his own personal development, in his words, an account of "events which impressed me with feelings which, from what I had been, have made me what I am." The monster is the one character in the novel who changes and develops. He does not remain the same. Contemporary science fiction is often faulted for its deep sense of science and shallow sense of character, but it is worth remembering that science fiction began by asking basic questions about the formation of human character. How is it formed? How stable is it? How does it develop over time?

The *Star Trek* series often returns to some of the unrealized possibilities for the genre seen above in *Frankenstein*. Indeed, as we shall often see, it is very much in the nature of *Star Trek* to extend the ordinary boundaries of science fiction. Where many other science fictions give us monsters, *Star Trek* gives us fully realized alien cultures like the Klingons. Where many other science fictions aim at an epic sweep, *Star Trek* exhibits an uncanny mastery of minute detail. And where many other science fictions draw character in broad external outlines, *Star Trek* gives us a thorough examination of the inner lives of its major characters. This chapter will show that the series tries to address many of the questions about character and identity raised by the very first science fiction novel. *Frankenstein* is, above all, a study of character under intense pressure. Science plays a minimal role in this first work of science fiction; Mary Shelley races through Dr. Frankenstein's calculations in a very few sentences. The creation scene featured in so many movies takes up only a few pages in the novel. Shelley's interest is not in the impact of Frankenstein's scientific discovery on humanity; his scientific secrets die with the monster. Her interest is in the formation and deformation of character; throughout the novel the monster is a character in search of an identity. His sense of identity is threatened and always insecure, for he is being hunted down like an animal. A large part of the book is actually told from the point of view of the monster himself.

A large number of *Star Trek* episodes are likewise seen from the perspective of one individual character. The difference is that, in *Star Trek,* most characters do not actually develop over time. They are who they are, and we see them acting in characteristic ways as we move from episode to episode. Picard is a private man with scholarly interests; Riker pursues women; Worf is immersed in his Klingon culture. In this series each character has a strong core sense of identity. Identity is something they already have, not something they are in search of, but something they possess and can lose. Identity is a given that can be taken. In *Star Trek* we sense who these characters are not because we see them developing but because we see them losing their identity and trying to get it back again. What we see again and again in the series is not the discovery of identity but its loss and recovery.

The loss of identity takes many forms and occupies a great many episodes. The loss can sometimes take the form of a substitution, where alien forces simply replace the personality, or a duality, where two different personalities, the old and the new, coexist within the character and contend for supremacy. The second scenario is far and away the most common plot dealing with identity in *Star Trek.* A character suddenly starts to multiply; he finds that he is not one but two people, or two coexisting beings who have to sort things out. The double of the self usually assumes one of three forms: a twin, an alien possession, or a duality of consciousness. Twins are particularly common in the series. At different times we get two Kirks, two Rikers, and two Picards; an episode of the original series, "Mirror, Mirror," goes so far as to create a twin for every character on the ship. Aliens also intervene to cloud identity, as in "Frame of Mind," where Riker is spirited away to an alien insane asylum, and existing selves often merge, as in "Attached," where Picard and Beverly Crusher are forced to inhabit a common consciousness. Perhaps half the episodes in the series involve some kind of identity loss. The series is immensely imaginative in devising alter egos for its characters. But in each case the multiplication is not smooth; there is a struggle between the selves as each character fights to retain his identity against the incursion. At times the series can even seem to push its characters to the edge of schizophrenia.

Why is the self always so threatened in *Star Trek*? Why is the series so determined to subvert the identity of its major characters? The answer, as we shall see, lies in *Star Trek*'s conception of the individual self.

1

Star Trek can be relentless in its valuation of the single human life. The series begins with an often-unexamined premise: that individuals must develop to their fullest possible extent, and to their fullest possible capacity. This idea may seem unimpeachable, but look again. The corridors of the *Enterprise* are full of talented and accomplished people who do not let anything get in their way. The characters do their jobs almost perfectly, but this perfection comes at a price. Few, if any, can maintain a lasting connection with others, other than friendship. Their duty and loyalty is primarily to the ship, and despite the network of friendships pervading the ship, they have little success in forging family connections. Even worse, as we shall see, the series kills off families at a rapid rate. Space exploration seems to preclude human reproduction, or at least lead to a strict division of labor between explorers and colonists, who interact but seldom intermarry. Few, if any, of the crew members of the *Enterprise* engage in romantic liaisons with people who have a nesting instinct, and when they do, the consequences are immediately disastrous.

A typical moment comes at the beginning of "Silicon Avatar." Commander Riker is on the surface of Omicron Theta helping a group of colonists survey their new home. The planet is lush, green, and fertile. He is having a conversation with Carmen Davila, a very pretty woman. They are contrasting their lives. Riker tells her how much it means to him to be a member of a ship exploring the galaxy. She tells him that her goal is to make a home and have a family, transforming this empty planet into a settled and familiar place. For a moment Riker softens. He is usually a womanizer, but her account strikes a chord in him and he agrees to have dinner with her. A different kind of life seems to appear before him, a life with a wife and children. But not for long. Almost as soon as he has this vision of himself as living in a community, a crystalline entity descends from the sky, turning everything in its path into stone. The colonists try to flee, but Carmen alone is touched by the entity and turned into a lattice of quartz. The connection between the conversation and the attack is not meant to be causal, but it is more than coincidental. Riker sees his dream of a wife and family shattered before his very eyes.

The turning of Carmen Davila into stone may be taken as a symbol for what *Star Trek* does to families. The series is not kind to families; it turns them too into stone. None of the major characters in *The Next Generation* comes from a stable family background. Picard violated his father's wishes by entering Starfleet Academy and was effectively disowned by him. Riker's mother died when he was two and he was raised intermittently by his father, Kyle Riker, who abandoned him at fifteen and from whom he is estranged as an adult. Worf's parents were both killed in the Khitomer massacre, and he was raised as an adopted child by a Russian couple on earth. He managed to have a son, Alexander Roshenko, but the series immediately killed off the mother, K'Ehleyr, after only one episode. Dr. Crusher is a widow and single mother. Geordi La Forge has two parents, career Starfleet officers who were never together as a complete couple on the same planet long enough to raise him. Ensign Ro Laren had to watch the Cardassians torture her father to death. Tasha Yar was raised on the streets of a planet teeming with rape gangs, and her very name evokes the Nazi massacre of Jewish families at Babi Yar in Russia. Guinan has no distinct parentage, but she too was raised on the run, her entire people forced into general exile by the Borg. The fact is unavoidable: every major character on *Star Trek* comes from a broken or fragmented home.

The series also leaves a trail of unsuccessful relationships. Riker and Troi were once lovers and are now friends. Worf's son is the issue of a very short and turbulent relationship. Picard and Crusher often veer toward romantic involvement but hold off, each too private to engage fully with the other. The remoteness and privacy of Captain Picard, the main character in *The Next Generation,* may be taken as a kind of ideal offered by the series. The loneliness of command is a figure for the loneliness and isolation of the discrete individual in command of himself. Episodes often end with Picard standing near a window, lost in his own thoughts, staring into the vastness of space. Space exploration often seems to lead to this quintessential *Next Generation* moment where the lone individual meditates on his position in space. Even the layout of the *Enterprise* mirrors this extreme individualism. Usually ship's quarters are compact and crowded spaces. But on the *Enterprise* the hallways are wide and nearly empty, and each crew member has a suite of rooms. Their rooms are never close to each other; the *Enterprise* is not like a dormitory with Picard next to Riker next to Worf. The *Enterprise* is laid out as if each of its characters had the floor of a hotel to himself, as if each individual were surrounded by a kind of buffer zone insulating him from the others.

Why this extreme isolation of individuals? The answer is that *Star Trek* values the individual at the expense of all groups, even the small group constituted by the couple or the family. The point is made over and over again. Picard gives so many speeches extolling the virtues of individual freedom and autonomy that in one episode, "True Q," Q interrupts him and says he has heard it all before, and besides, Picard does not really understand what he is saying. In a way Q is right. The series gives maximum autonomy to each of its characters, but that autonomy comes at a price. The main characters in *Star Trek* are too concerned with themselves and their careers to form intimate family ties with others. The heightened development of the individual, perhaps the primary value of the series, often leads to the effective isolation of the individual, even in the midst of a starship crew.

The emphasis on the individual can often turn up in unexpected places. Time travel, for instance, is common in *Star Trek*. In most other science fiction time travel evokes the largest possible scope of historical process. In H. G. Wells's *The Time Machine,* the journey through time takes us to a far point in the future when civilization as we know it no longer exists, when only the contour of the land is as it was. A number of episodes of *Star Trek* follow this pattern in skipping back and forth over the vast reaches of time; one, "All Good Things," even takes us back to see the beginnings of life on earth. The series worries constantly about the implications of time travel, which are called "disruptions of the space-time continuum." This sounds pretty vast, but in practice the "disruptions" are much smaller. In "Tapestry" Q takes Picard back in time to relive certain choices he made as a young cadet at Starfleet Academy. The premise of a time travel episode in *Star Trek* is always that the modification of a single life can change history. In *Star Trek* time travel episodes every life matters, every life is precious. Individual will and action are always more important than collective will and action. Despite the vastness of time, time conforms to the outline of a single human life. Time is wound around a human clock.

Star Trek can sometimes push individual autonomy to incredible extremes. In "Man of the People" Picard makes a revealing decision. The *Enterprise* has been carrying an ambassador named Ves Alkar to mediate a conflict on a war-torn planet. Alkar is a man surrounded by a resonant calm, which he uses to settle disputes. But it turns out that he is a kind of parasite who derives his composure by draining others of theirs. In the first act his host, an old woman, dies, and he attaches himself to Deanna Troi, who then rapidly begins to age. But Alkar uses her energy to good ends. He sets himself to negotiating a peace on the warring planet. Deanna is now dying, but the ambassador is using her energy to conclude negotiations and save millions of lives. Captain Picard soon discovers the transfer of energy and is faced with a quandary. If the ambassador is successful, he will have saved millions of lives, but he will have killed Deanna. For a moment Picard has to hold in the balance two competing interests: the interests of one human life and the interests of three billion people. He does not hesitate. Deanna must live and the planet must die. He severs the tie between the ambassador and Troi and Deanna returns to normal.

In this episode Picard does not actually have to go through with his threat, but he makes it clear that he is willing to act on principle. That principle is that no one, under no circumstances, has the right to abrogate the freedom of the individual. This particular episode avoids confronting the consequences of this decision, and Picard does not have to condemn a planet to death to save one woman. His decision and its consequences would have been more striking had Picard simply seized Troi earlier and left the planet to its fate. But even his choice on principle stands as a symbol for a choice the series makes over and over again. The individual is paramount, the group secondary.

The situation in "Man of the People" is extreme in some ways but representative in others. *Star Trek* recognizes that individuality comes at a price, and the series is forever running its characters through situations in which they must confront the limits of individual autonomy. These situations vary widely. One character may be shown the family he never had, while another may be spirited away to a cell in which he is made to confront the prison of the self. There is even a nightmare scenario in which the characters on the *Enterprise* devolve into different extinct animal species who have absolutely nothing in common. In each of these situations characters suffer removal from the *Enterprise* to have their very identities thrown into question. The most extreme version of this plot questioning identity actually creates a double of the character, another Kirk, another Riker, another Data, usually a mirror image or an opposite, calling into question not only the autonomy but also the uniqueness of the solitary individual.

The most basic ties we have to other people are usually family ties, and though most of the major characters in the series are childless, family ties often appear indirectly in *Star Trek*. A very common plot in *The Next Generation* involves unwelcome visits from family members. This plot is very predictable. The *Enterprise* stops somewhere and an unexpected visitor beams on board. It may be Kyle Riker, come to pressure his son to accept a promotion to captain, or it may be Nikolai Roshenko, Worf's stepbrother, come to recruit the *Enterprise* for a humanitarian mission. Whoever the visitor, no crew member is ever glad to receive a family member on board. The crew of the *Enterprise* never look forward to these visits, which are often unexpected, and when they come, they often spell trouble. The typical visiting family member is well intentioned, self-absorbed, and meddlesome. *The Next Generation* makes Lwaxana Troi into the perfect representative of this role. Lwaxana is, as she keeps reminding her daughter Deanna, "Keeper of the Rings of the Seventh House of Betazed and Daughter of the Royal House of Troi." She repeats this ridiculous title like a mantra throughout the ten episodes in which she appears. Lwaxana is a parody of a mother. Her name implies that she is behaving improperly for her age, waxing rather than waning. Her sexuality is out of control and she propositions nearly every man she meets. In most episodes Deanna must care for her instead of the other way around. After a time, Lwaxana's presence becomes a standing joke in the series: whenever she appears, the other characters scatter and think of ways to get her off the ship.

In many ways Lwaxana Troi is an emblem of family ties as seen by the series. Part of space exploration in *Star Trek* seems to involve getting away from family members like Lwaxana Troi. She is seen in high form in an episode called "Cost of Living." In this episode Lwaxana beams on board and announces that she is going to get married to a man she has never met. Of course when she finally meets her intended, he turns out to be a stodgy and dour man. But Lwaxana has something of the strong individual bent seen throughout the series. Even though she does not like her fiancé, she decides to go through with her wedding anyway, showing up naked for the ceremony, forcing it to be cancelled. But there is more to the episode than a called-off wedding. The episode couples Lwaxana's search for a husband with a revealing subplot. As Lwaxana courts her chosen mate, a colony of metallic parasites is slowly eating away at the ship's bulkheads. These parasites were picked up just about the time Lwaxana beamed on board, and Data manages to clear the ship of them just about the time she leaves. The episode makes no direct connection between its two plots, but there are a number of suggestive parallels. Both Deanna's mother and the parasites are unwelcome visitors. They both feed off the ship, and everyone is glad to see them go. It is as if Lwaxana too is a kind of parasite, living off the life of her daughter when her daughter should be living a life of her own. The symbolic implication is clear: family acts like a parasite on the free individual. In "Cost of Living" Lwaxana Troi chooses a husband almost randomly; the implication is that family is something you can never choose. Since the characters live in a universe where free will and individual choice are paramount, family is bound to fly in the face of individual autonomy. The Federation itself, as it never tires of proclaiming, is a voluntary confederation of worlds. *Star Trek* always prefers voluntary confederation to involuntary ones, and this preference extends to the most involuntary confederation of all, the family.

Family ties are often the subject of comedy in *Star Trek,* so much so that it is easy to conclude that the series does not take families seriously. Indeed, with the exception of *Star Trek: Voyager,* where the crew is lost in space, the series entirely omits the most common human response to extended journeys: homesickness. The great navies of the world have always had to contend with homesickness as a serious factor affecting morale. Most movies about navies feature scenes of sailors pining for home. But there is no letter writing or calls home on the *Enterprise.* Family is what they left behind; crew members are never homesick; crew are more likely to be shown avidly pursuing their individual interests and hobbies. The implication is that these are career Starfleet officers and that their home is the ship. The reason for this lack of sentiment is not hard to ascertain. The family is a direct threat to the autonomy of the individual. In the series families are seen not to enhance but to restrict the range of individual freedom. The emphasis, as we will see again and again, is on extending the individual, not on consolidating the group. Group consciousness is more likely to be represented as the worst possible thing in the universe, as in the case of the Borg.

The series may not take real families seriously, but it takes imaginary ones very seriously. Real families are likely to be the subject of comedy, and we often see the crew of the *Enterprise* wincing with embarrassment at the buffoonery of their relatives. Imaginary families are fantasies of families as experienced by different characters, and the feeling in these episodes is often more tragic than comic. The fantasy of the family takes many forms in *Star Trek.* As noted above, in no case in either series do major characters meet, mate, and procreate. But the series is uncannily aware of those aspects of human experience it normally excludes from its usual operations, and it labors to include them as elaborate fantasies, so that procreative family fantasies fill the series. A woman without children may be made to experience pregnancy, childbirth, the birth and death of a child. A man without children is often suddenly provided with a family. In one episode Deanna Troi is impregnated by a space incubus. In another Geordi La Forge is seen in the future as a married man with three children. Sometimes these fantasies have the effect of immunizing these characters against further fantasies. In the two above instances, after the events of "The Child," we hear little more of Deanna Troi's desire for a child, and the scenes in "All Good Things" showing Geordi as a married man are revealed to be part of a future that may never happen, and in any case the series ends before we really know. But unquestionably the most highly developed family fantasy in the series surrounds Jean-Luc Picard, the captain of the *Enterprise*. Alone among the major characters of the series, Captain Picard seems the most resistant to family life and, as such, he is often singled out to experience the family ties he never had.

The Next Generation begins with Picard's denial of family ties. Just a few minutes into "Encounter at Farpoint" we see Picard frowning at some children he sees, distinctly uncomfortable with the idea of families aboard the *Enterprise*. He wants them off the bridge and confined to certain decks of the ship. A few episodes try and nudge him up against children a bit more closely, as in "Disaster," where he is trapped in a broken turbolift with three children who have just won prizes at a science fair. Others go much farther, providing him with a wife, a family, even a full-grown son. In the first series James T. Kirk was sometimes provided with a wife and children, but usually as part of an amnesiac episode where his memory as a starship captain has been wiped clean, as in "The Paradise Syndrome." In striking contrast Picard is provided with experiences he remembers, and even more importantly, experiences specifically designed for him to remember them. In its pursuit of rounded character *Star Trek* is forever probing the absent spaces in the lives of its major characters. A sort of principle of negative space plays a very large role in imagining character in the series: the series explores not only who and what they are but who and what they are not—and who and what they could have been.

2

An episode called "The Inner Light" offers by far the most elaborate family fantasy in the series. En route to Starbase 218 after
completing a survey of magnetic waves, the *Enterprise* encounters
an alien object—a probe—drifting in space. The probe ignores or
bypasses everyone on the bridge but Picard, going straight for him,
and after a flaring of color, the bridge of the *Enterprise* dissolves and
Picard finds himself in a deep overstuffed chair, a woman standing
over him, blotting his forehead with a damp towel.

This woman is his wife. He is apparently home, wherever that is.
His first response is to say, "Computer, freeze program. End program." Picard clearly thinks that this is another holodeck fantasy,
and he is telling the computer he wants it to end. But it does not
end. Eline still stands over him, smiling radiantly, telling him he's
feverish. This is clearly not going to be another holodeck fantasy
episode where a character gets caught inside a story not of his own
making (more on this in the next chapter). Picard is not going to
play at being Sherlock Holmes or Beowulf. The immediate sense
we get is that Picard is not going to experience a story drawn from
elsewhere. What he is about to experience is a story intrinsic to
himself, a story he can no more shut off than he can shut down his
own mind. The alien intervention of the probe has carried him off
somewhere, but not away from himself or into some other story,
just more deeply into himself.

The interest of "The Inner Light" is that he lives out another life
that turns out to be as viable as his own. Picard has awakened to
find himself called Kamin. He lives in a small villa, part of a village
that appears to border on a vast desert. He finds that he is well
known in the village as Kamin, known not because of any profes-

sional position but because he is a good friend and neighbor. So it is not Kamin's public position that matters much in "The Inner Light." Everything in the episode is intensely private. From act to act the episode covers nearly twenty years of Picard's life as Kamin. At one point his wife tells him that his other existence as a starship captain must have been extraordinary, "but never once, in all the stories you've told me, have you mentioned anyone who loved you as I do." She has a point. Usually in *The Next Generation* Picard's life as a Starfleet officer is almost wholly taken up with his career. Though he has personal interests, he has few close friends, certainly nothing to rival the friendships of Data and Geordi or Riker and Worf. The events in Picard's life as a Starfleet officer are part of a very public record of Starfleet history, and he is always meeting strangers who are familiar with the story of his incarceration by the Borg or his torture by the Cardassians. Even his hobbies, though eccentric, are social and involve things like giving papers at archaeological conferences. Though a private man, he has almost no truly private existence.

"The Inner Light" gives him a private life and a private love, things lacking in his life aboard the *Enterprise.* At first we see only Kamin and Eline, but after five years they decide to start a family. The episode is full of private events in the life of his family. Throughout the episode the essential privacy of that life is seen in Kamin's flute playing. He plays the flute not in preparation for an expert public performance of the kind often seen in the *Enterprise* amphitheater but simply for his own enjoyment. This sense of a private choice is mirrored in the choice of career made by Kamin's son. His son decides not to pursue a public career as a scientist or a public servant, but instead to follow his own leanings, whether he is suited to them or not, and become a musician like his father. This again is something almost never seen on *Star Trek:* children following in the footsteps of their parents. Usually there is a basic disruption of the family from generation to generation; in very few instances indeed do the family of any major character live on any one planet, or pursue anything like the same profession. Family is scattered and paternity is discontinuous.

But there is a shadow over the world of family on the planet Kataan. The world is slowly coming to an end. As Kamin, Picard soon realizes that the planet is doomed. Kamin has to continue life much as he has been living it, aware now that the time remaining for life on this planet is limited. The older he gets, the more he has to confront the fact that his children will not be able to live out complete lives on Kataan.

Lived under the pall of such immense coming destruction, each action takes on a heightened significance. Putting on a shoe, adjusting the brim of a hat, playing the flute: everything he does now becomes something that will come to an end soon. At the very end of the episode he takes his daughter and grandson to the launching of a rocket—the probe that, a thousand years in the future, will find a starship captain named Jean-Luc Picard and allow him to experience the course of a life on the planet Kataan. "The rest of us have been gone for a thousand years," Eline tells him. Picard awakens on the bridge of the *Enterprise,* having lived out another life in a very short time. He is now the only person in the universe who remembers that this people and this culture ever existed.

"The Inner Light" is told with great compression, and in a single episode Picard is provided with a happy family life. But even this happy life is lived out under the threat of imminent, catastrophic destruction. Picard knows that his children will not be able to live out full lives. A happy family life such as seen here is brief and fleeting; not only is there is a lingering air of tragedy about the whole episode, but there is also a pervasive sense of dislocation.

Throughout the episode Picard remembers that he was once someone else. As Kamin, Picard disappears for weeks at a time, wandering the mountains in search of a remembered identity that manages to elude him. Picard is never fully at ease in his new identity as Kamin, and again and again we see him trying to break out of it, going off alone, observing the universe through a telescope, taking an interest in large diplomatic matters, and arguing with the government administrator. This entire life represents a road not chosen, a path he chose not to pursue during his life with Starfleet. Taken as a parable about Picard's sense of family, "The Inner Light" is very revealing. His life with Eline takes place a thousand years in the past, just before the sun of their solar system goes supernova. His happy world is both distant and threatened. Family is in the past and family is doomed.

Correspondingly, the episode's emphasis on the individual could not be more pronounced. The dying planet does not send an archive into outer space containing a record of its history and achievements. Nor does it send a time capsule containing a selection of its documents and artifacts. It sends a probe directly into the mind of Picard. The rest of the crew of the *Enterprise* do not share in the experience, and in later episodes of the series Picard makes no attempt to tell them about it. From time to time Picard takes his flute out of its case, clearly cherishing it as among his most private memories. He is not even instructed to communicate that memory to others as a sort of messenger. At the very end of the episode Eline tells him not to pass on what he has seen but simply to remember it himself. "If *you* remember what we were and how we lived," she tells him, "then we'll have found life again."

It certainly seems a strange way for a culture to keep its memory alive. The Kataan culture seems to have asked only that its memory be brought alive again not for all time but for a relatively brief instant, the span of Picard's life. Picard too will ultimately die, but for the time he is alive he will carry within him the inner being of the culture he has experienced, then it too will die with him. As a device to preserve the memory of a lost culture, the probe would seem to be a senseless failure.

But if, for a moment, we view "The Inner Light" less as a story about the planet Kataan than as a story about Picard, the episode makes far greater sense. The implication throughout "The Inner Light" is that a single individual such as Jean-Luc Picard is capable of carrying the memory of an entire culture. The memory may not survive him, but the fact remains: for a time Picard and Picard alone is the carrier of an entire culture. Just as important is the fact that the essential experiences of that culture are intimate and completely incommunicable. As Kamin, Picard does not load up on stories such as mythical tales to bring back to the *Enterprise*. Those stories are generally how a culture chooses to represent itself, and they can frequently be misleading, as in the various Klingon myths about Kahless, or difficult to understand, as in "Darmok." But the experience of the Kataan culture is fully Picard's and Picard's alone. "Now we live," Eline tells him in the last moments of the episode, "in you."

It may seem that here, yet again, *Star Trek* has once again annihilated the family and exaggerated the importance of the single individual. Lest we think that the series has gone too far, it is worth remembering that there is a real historical truth in this essential incommunicability of culture. Historians frequently write about how hard it is to get beyond the names and dates of history; a culture's sense of itself usually dies with the culture, and rare indeed is the historian who can piece together the existence of a culture from the inside out. Picard's experience of recovering the inner existence of a lost culture is every historian's dream. Today the discipline of history has moved beyond a concern with the external and most public realms of human experience, the stately procession of rulers and governments and wars, often choosing to focus instead on the minute details of everyday life, the diurnal rhythms of family, work, and friendship. "The Inner Light" is a kind of testament to the overlooked details of everyday life. It shows that life can often escape the scrutinizing gaze of historical memory. Nobody else will ever remember Picard's life as Kamin with anything like the fullness with which Picard remembers it. Nevertheless that memory contains within itself the essential experiences of the Kataan culture. The troubling implication of "The Inner Light" is that cultures do not always succeed in remembering, let alone recording, their most important experiences. Many of the most characteristic features of any culture die with that culture, never to be successfully communicated to posterity. The inner light burning within Picard may be the light of the Kataan culture, but nobody else will ever see it. The interest of "The Inner Light" is that it takes Picard's life and fills it not with a vast public archive but with private moments that could only hold meaning for him and his family alone.

The episode also makes one remarkable omission. The people on the planet have no name. Indeed "The Inner Light" is the only episode in nearly three hundred episodes of *Star Trek* in which an alien people lack a name for themselves. *The Star Trek Encyclopedia* feels obliged to make up a name for them, the Ressikans, but that name never appears in the episode. The omission is revealing. Names of peoples are usually how they are known not to themselves but to others. Overwhelmingly, the peoples of the world have different names for themselves than those others have devised for them. An example is Sioux, which is a lump term invented by white settlers to designate the Plains Indians, who of course knew themselves by their individual tribal names. The reason Picard learns no name for this people is that the name of a people is inherently a public thing, while Picard is experiencing the private *inner* being of a people. They pass their inner memory to Picard without transmitting to him any external structures whatsoever. Their political structure remains hazy, as do their cultural accomplishments. They appear to have no special technology. All Picard learns is that this is the community of Ressik, located in the Northern Province of a planet called Kataan. They are not known categorically to him as Ressikans but simply as individuals living in a tightly knit community of families.

So in its way *Star Trek* does take family ties seriously. In "The Inner Light" we are a long way from the comedy of Lwaxana Troi's visits to the *Enterprise.* The episode equips Picard with a family, and even more importantly, a happy family. Stories about happiness are rare in *Star Trek,* as well as everywhere else. From Aristotle onward, it is a staple of literary criticism that unhappiness is a more likely subject for stories than happiness. The consensus is that conflict is easier to represent than harmony because harmony is self-directed and conflict is other-directed. Even our most basic words about plot and character reveal something about the turmoil we expect in our characters and their stories. The main character of a story is called a protagonist, which comes from the Greek word *agon,* from which we derive our word "agony." In our tradition the hero of a typical story is a person in agony. Suffering is a very common theme in Western literature, while happiness is almost absent. Even *Star Trek* is not immune from this tradition. The "trouble in utopia" plot, analyzed above, views happy societies with suspicion; they almost always turn out to be repressive and the crew of the *Enterprise* must take action to break them apart. Seen in the context of this tradition, "The Inner Light" performs a very remarkable operation. It shows a happy life, a life fully lived out in a balanced society. It offers far and away the most convincing portrait of marital and family love seen in the series. A happily married couple is usually an object of suspicion in the series, as in "The Survivors," where a retired couple, Rishon and Kevin Uxbridge, are the lone survivors of a planet-wide catastrophe; in this episode their intimacy becomes a kind of conspiracy, for they conceal the truth about the end of their world from Federation investigators. But in "The Inner Light" the love between Picard and Eline is evident and deepens as the episode progresses. The scene where they decide to have children has the very beat of intimacy. The christening scene, where they publicly declare their love for each other and their family, has no hint of satire and has no equal in the series.

"The Inner Light," then, represents something like a wish-fulfillment dream for Picard. The wish-fulfillment dream is sometimes misunderstood. A wish-fulfillment dream is not necessarily a dream for something we actually want in our waking life. It is simply a dream for something we do not have and may never have. In his life as a Starfleet officer Picard does not regret his actions; in one episode, "Tapestry," Q takes him back into the past and Picard winds up admitting that, given the chance, he would do much the same thing over again. A wish-fulfillment dream, rather, is a dream of something unattainable, a dream seeking to fill the absent spaces in our lives. These dreams function to alert us to the choices we have made, and to accustom us to them. Picard is acutely aware that, at the age of fifty-one, he is unlikely to start a family. The reason he is surrounded by projections of possible families is that his choice really is final. He will have no children. Another dream of this sort, seen comparably through a kind of haze lens, appears in *Star Trek: Generations,* the seventh *Star Trek* film, where Picard is made to experience a Christmas holiday with the family he will never have.

In each of these cases the dream functions to adjust Picard to choices he has made in his real life as captain of the starship *Enterprise*.

The wish-fulfillment dream is a desirable thing, and seen in the right light, so is Picard's second self in "The Inner Light." Indeed the episode offers a remarkable take on the splitting of the self so often seen in the series. Doubles in *Star Trek* are usually undesirable evil twins (I will deal with them shortly), and they almost always need to be driven away for the self to return to normal. But here Picard's double does not split his personality but augments it. The life he experiences as Kamin actually supplements his own. The episode reads like a recitation of what *The Next Generation* leaves out of his life. These are all family moments, such as a quiet moment with his wife, a talk with his son about his choice of career, a walk with his granddaughter. There is the birth of a son and the death of a friend. The second life Picard lives out adds a whole new dimension to his life, eliciting qualities seldom seen in the captain of the *Enterprise*. Picard is usually compassionate but not tender, engaged but not involved. As Kamin, he widens the scope of his identity; quite remarkably, the temporary loss of identity sometimes turns out to be a gain. In "The Inner Light," as in *Star Trek* generally, identity seems often to be enhanced by its temporary loss. The reconstructed self turns out to be stronger than the initially constructed one. The confrontation with the alien forces of the mind strengthens the inner being of character and takes it in new directions. Following his encounter with the Borg, Picard returns to earth and forges new connections with his family. His own experience of having a family in "The Inner Light" makes him more sympathetic to the presence of families aboard the *Enterprise*. Amazingly enough, a multiplication of selves inside a character does not necessarily lead to schizophrenia and madness. It can lead to an enhanced sense of selfhood in which an individual becomes aware of the presence of other lives within and around him. The individual becomes aware of himself not as an isolated entity but as a source of social multiplicity, effectively countering the tendency of the series toward the isolation of individuals.

But the "The Inner Light" goes even farther, offering a new take on the multiple personality. As Kamin, Picard remembers that he was once someone else, a man with a vast scope of action and interaction. This memory fades somewhat as the episode progresses, but it haunts him until the moment when the tie between him and the planet Kataan is severed and he returns to normal on the *Enterprise*. The sense here is that Picard *needs* the exposure to this other life, he needs to see what was in him to become. The double life he leads as Kamin may be an illusion, for Picard obviously did not live out this life a thousand years previous in a place he has never been, but it is a necessary illusion. It reminds him of what has made him what he is. In "The Inner Light" it is as if Picard comes to see himself, and value himself, from another point of view. He needs both of these lives at once, and the more we know him, the more that we see that he is actually both of these people. There is no Jekyll-and-Hyde effect; Picard needs Kamin and Kamin needs Picard. The beauty of "The Inner Light" is that it creates a double for Picard who is worthy of him. Kamin really does show what Picard would be like under different circumstances. He is a viable double; his life does not try to replace Picard's but instead supplements it in vital ways. Picard, it seems, is not one but many.

The same point is made somewhat more crudely in "The Enemy Within," an episode of the original series. In this episode there has been yet another transporter malfunction. The transporter has split Kirk into two different captains of the *Enterprise*. The civilized Kirk is calm, measured, and introspective. The savage Kirk is the picture of excess. He drinks heavily and tries to rape Yeoman Janice Rand. He craves power and regards the ship not as a command bestowed by others but as his own personal possession. At first the civilized Kirk tries to retain command of the *Enterprise,* but he finds he has lost the faculty of command. He is indecisive and unsure of himself; the only thing he knows for sure is that he wants this duplication of himself to be kept a secret. But as usual in *Star Trek,* the question of identity is a public question, perhaps the most public question of all, and the status of James T. Kirk quickly becomes a matter of shipwide concern. At first the savage Kirk tries to kill the civilized Kirk, but soon they find they need one another because they are the separated halves of the same self. As Scotty readies the transporter, there is a wonderful image of Kirk hugging his alter ego as he prepares to reunite with him. There is tension, hatred, separation, but also love and need. Of course Scotty's rigging of the transporter is successful. They come together and James T. Kirk is James T. Kirk again, but this doubling seen in "The Enemy Within" remains wonderfully mirrored in his very name. Kirk comes from a Scotch word for "church" and evokes the array of laws by which social institutions such as the church have traditionally regulated the self. But the middle initial of his name stands for Tiberius, the first-century Roman emperor known for his excesses and debaucheries. James Tiberius Kirk goes back to being himself, but that self, as seen in the case of Jean-Luc Picard, is divided by definition.

This process of supplementing a character from within is basic to the series. Human beings are social multiples whether they like it or not. The series sees the individual as many things at once, held together like planets by the gravitational force of a single star. The title of *The Next Generation* episode—"The Inner Light"—effectively brings home this need for social multiplicity. An inner light is usually taken to be a spirit of inspiration or composure coming from inside the individual. That is, an inner light is usually taken to originate from within. But in this episode an inner light is also a light ignited inside an individual by the action of a probe coming from outside. In "The Inner Light" the light is both Picard's and that of the probe. The double meaning of the image implies that the inner sanctum of the self, the sanctuary where the inner light burns, is not a private and isolated place. Deep within Picard is not only the inner light of himself but also the inner light of an entire culture, its hopes, dreams, family structure, and religious mores. The most private place of all turns out to be the most deeply social. Inside Picard, with a fullness he can scarcely communicate to anyone else, is an entire culture. There is no mediative stillness at the heart of the self, but a busy social world full of comings and goings, marriages, children, life and death. "The Inner Light" serves to remind us that each individual is a crucible of culture. The series may do everything it can to preserve the integrity of the individual, but the individual is integral for a surprising reason. No man is an island because each man is a continent.

3

This remarkable perception, that the individual is social to the core, accounts for certain attitudes pervading a number of other episodes. *Star Trek* does not look kindly on meditation or other cloistered-up spiritual activities. It sees them as quietistic and life-denying. Spock pursues a rigorous Vulcan spiritual discipline that he must renounce in order to help the Federation make peace with the Klingon Empire. Lieutenant Worf tries his hand at Klingon spiritual exercises only to find, in "Kahless," that the high priests of the Klingon religion have been perpetuating a fraud. In both these cases the individual is in danger of becoming too isolated, worshipping at the votive flame of the self. As we shall see in the last chapter of this book, "The Sense of Wonder," *Star Trek*'s inclinations are always far more deeply social; magical experiences are mostly shared experiences, not private ones. The series looks down on characters who purse religious disciplines solely for their own profit. The sense throughout is that the core of the self must remain socially engaged to remain healthy and whole.

The series treats the social engagement of the self as something more than an article of pop psychology. Freud once said that the social engagement of the self comes at a great cost; we must repress our antisocial urges, transforming them into compulsions, driving them into the realm of the unconscious mind. The recognition that the social self has unconscious counterparts in the personality leads the series to create unconscious counterparts, or doubles, for many of its major characters. Very few characters in *Star Trek* escape doubling. The division of the self is usually pretty simple: one half of the self is socially engaged, the other is socially disengaged. One is external; the other is internal. One is socially adjusted; one is socially destructive. This can be seen in virtually every case of twins offered by the series. Data serves aboard the *Enterprise,* while his evil twin, Lore, is incubated in isolation. Riker is commander, while his double, Thomas, remains stranded and in complete isolation for eight years on Rema Three. Even in episodes where the entire crew is somehow doubled, the same principle obtains. In "Mirror, Mirror," an episode of the original series, the doubles of the crew become a crew of pirates ravaging the quadrant in their galaxy-class starship. In *Star Trek* the twin is always the isolated double of the self. The twin is there to show what life is like in a world where the mind is free of social obligation and constraint. Twins in *Star Trek* typically do whatever they want and are unconcerned with the consequences of their actions. They are examples of the self in danger of sliding into solipsism, or the state in which one person is convinced that he is the only person there is. Twins are necessarily the delusional doubles of the self, in the series almost all twins suffer from delusions of grandeur. Lore thinks he can single-handedly unite the Borg against the Federation. Thomas Riker thinks he can single-handedly tilt the balance of power toward a beleaguered guerrilla organization called the Maquis. Kirk's double is a megalomaniac concerned only with murdering his enemies and amassing personal power. The characters who are doubled vary from episode to episode, but the doubles themselves act with great regularity. The double in *Star Trek* is always a projection of the asocial individual self, the individual sunk so deeply in himself that he refuses to recognize the existence of others, the solitary self spun out of control.

At first glance it might seem strange that a highly civilized milieu such as the starship *Enterprise* should be such a magnet for antisocial doubles. The *Enterprise* is, after all, a magnificent technological creation; the Federation it belongs to is, compared to our own world, positively serene. Why, then, are its corridors full of monstrous doubles of its major characters?

The answer lies in *Star Trek*'s very vision of social perfectability. As everyone knows, the series shows a much better world than the one we live in now, as well as a much better world than those seen in most science fiction. But a psychologist like Freud would view this better world as having been bought at a terrible price. According to Freud, the more civilized a culture becomes, the more deeply it drives its antisocial urges underground. Freud does not think that these violent urges ever disappear. Rather, they incubate for a time, unchecked and invisible, mutating like viruses and reappearing in new and ever more virulent form. According to Freud, the closer we get to creating a society in which those urges have no place, the more likely it is that these urges will seek and find new places for themselves. The characters of *Star Trek* may live in a world free from the social dislocation of poverty, prejudice, and hunger, but as Freud would say, they can never escape from the dislocation of unconscious forces that the very creation of that society has required. The series often recognizes the cost of civilization when it treats many of its most civilized characters with a basic suspicion. An externally civilized society in *Star Trek* often turns out to be internally barbaric, as in "The Masterpiece Society," where eugenic breeding is practiced, or "The Return of the Archons," where people are controlled by a malevolent machine. One recurring character in the series could be called "the malevolent ambassador," usually a cultured and civilized man who attains his calm by draining someone else of theirs, as in "Man of the People," analyzed earlier, where Ves Alkar nearly drains Deanna Troi dry. Gul Madred, Picard's torturer in "Chain of Command," is likewise a highly civilized man. Like Freud, *Star Trek* sees civilization as coming at a price; but even beyond Freud, the series often sees barbarism lurking under the polished veneer of civilized exteriors. There are no evil twins in the *Star Wars* movies, where evil itself plays such a prominent role.

This sense of lurking barbarism leads the series to create a special office for dealing with the problem. There was no staff psychologist on the original *Enterprise* (although Sally Kellerman made a pass at this role in the second series pilot), but in *The Next Generation* Counselor Deanna Troi fills a special function. She is there to keep the civilizing process intact, to deal with any problems impeding the rational operation of the *Enterprise*. The social adjustment of personality is the great goal of *Star Trek,* so much so that in *The Next Generation* the series created an adjustment office in the form of Deanna Troi's counseling chamber. Here her advice is always the same: "Don't worry, give it time, you'll adjust, you'll fit in." Fitting in is what most *Star Trek* plots are about; they are parables of identity, and Troi is often there at key moments to ratify them. Indeed it is fairly common for an episode of *The Next Generation* to end with a character debriefing Troi about his or her most personal experiences. At the end of his experience with the Cardassians, Picard tells her in a counseling session: "One thing I didn't put in my report . . ." What was not in his report will now go in her report. She is there to keep the self from being too private; Picard may not tell Starfleet, but he tells her. She is there to help in the readjustment of the self to social conditions. The truth of her function is revealed by the fact that officers are often required to attend sessions with her. Her title, counselor, evokes a blend of political and psychological functions. Even her name, Troi, means "third" in a number of languages and implies that she is the third, the interlocutor, in the unending dialogue of the self and its many doubles. Her special powers may be irrational, but they are always used for the most rational of ends. With Deanna Troi on board, there is ultimately no privacy on the *Enterprise;* as she is always saying, somewhat intrusively, "My office is always open to you." Through the offices of Counselor Troi, Starfleet is always eavesdropping on the lives of its characters.

The series, then, is always trying to micromanage the inner lives of its characters, adjusting them as best as possible to the demands of starship life. But sometimes the best efforts of Starfleet and Counselor Troi cannot prevent what often seems to be a massive breakdown of the self. These breakdowns are sudden and unexplained, and can often seem to push a character to the very brink of madness. We have already seen Picard abducted by aliens in one episode and penetrated by an alien probe in another. In "Frame of

Mind" Riker is spirited away to an alien mental asylum. In "Schisms" any number of crew members are transported to a different dimension, where they are subjected to alien medical experiments. The key word here is "alien." Threats to identity in *Star Trek* never come from within the characters themselves. No character is ever in danger of losing his mind for internal, psychological reasons. Threat to the integrity of the personality always turn out to come from the outside. Any number of episodes begin with characters wandering the corridors of the *Enterprise*, afraid they are losing their minds. Perhaps they are hallucinating; perhaps they think they are someone else; perhaps they think they are in two places at once. Riker is worn and haggard at the beginning of "Schisms"; Picard stumbles around the corridors in his bedclothes in "All Good Things." They appear to others to be deranged, paranoid, mad. But in every instance their derangement is fabricated, their paranoia justified, their madness induced. In every case aliens are to blame for their loss of themselves, and once the aliens are expelled, they return to normal after a painful process of self-reconstruction.

The fact that aliens so frequently go after human identity, however, leads me to conclude that alien forces are often stand-ins for the dark forces of the mind. The loss of identity happens in different ways to different characters. Each of them experiences alien possession in their own particular way. Very frequently these alien interventions have the effect of awakening the deepest and most unarticulated desires of the major characters: Picard's lack of family ties, Riker's sense that he is not in command of the *Enterprise* (and therefore of himself), Troi's sense of childlessness, Worf's suppressed drives toward violence. Though aliens are to blame for arousing these states, the states of mind themselves do not seem entirely alien to their personalities. Picard's son in "Bloodlines" may be an alien ruse, but his sense of childlessness is not. The same is true of Deanna Troi in "The Child," where an alien impregnates her with a child and the child lives out an entire life in the course of a single episode. Under alien influence the characters of *Star Trek* behave in ways that often articulate their deepest desires. Alien intervention disrupts the regulated world of character in *Star Trek,* the sensible world of behavioral evaluation represented by Counselor Deanna Troi's office, substituting in its place something like demonic possession. Centuries ago demons were often used as symbols for forces of the mind that people did not understand; demonic possession was an early way of explaining a multiple sense of selfhood. A similar process happens in *Star Trek:* we may never see the aliens causing a character to break down, or if we see them, they generally appear at the very end of an episode. What we do experience is the process of the breakdown itself, the moment-by-moment feeling that a character really is experiencing a loss of identity. The series calls this "alien intervention"; it was once called demonic possession. However you look at it, it represents the only real threat to the integrity of character seen in the series.

But the loss of identity always turns out to be temporary. For all the instances in the series, not one proves to be permanent. Dozens of other episodes end with the sense that characters will have to undergo a painful and laborious process of self-reconstruction before they can return to normal. But they always do return to normal. The series exorcises aliens every time. Even in the case of twins the strength of the individual turns out to be unbroken, and the twin usually suffers expulsion or death, allowing the character to resume his normal identity.

This scenario in which identity is lost and found has the effect of making characters in *Star Trek* seem a little too perfect, a little too complete. Picard is not destroyed or disabled by his experience of being mutilated by the Borg, as many war veterans are, but recovers and is reintegrated. The strength of the individual remains unbroken; to the end the series maintains the inner inviolability of the individual. The identities of the major characters are so strong and stable, in fact, that the producers of *The Next Generation* found it necessary to introduce a number of characters with unformed or incomplete identities. These characters are Wesley Crusher, Lieutenant Reginald Barclay, and Lieutenant Commander Data. Wesley is an adolescent, Barclay is a neurotic, and Data is an android. These characters act as foils to the others, for they exist in a state of perpetual incompletion and self-examination. These characters lack the inner sense of balance seen in most of the other major characters, who, in keeping with their need to maintain to maintain an perfectly functioning inner gyroscope, practice disciplines stressing inner and outer balance like the martial arts, fencing, and a Klingon form of Tai Chi (Worf, Troi, Crusher, Picard, and Guinan all regularly participate in these activities). In contrast these unformed characters are awkward and ofen clumsy. They have not yet learned the art of synchronizing their inner lives to the outer life represented by Starfleet. The episodes featuring them uniformly stress their social integration into the crew. In "Hollow Pursuits" Barclay must learn to overcome his isolation and make friends on the ship. In "The First Duty" Wesley must learn to behave in a way befitting a Starfleet officer. The implication is that they become fully normal only when they have completely assimilated Starfleet's norms, regulations, and codes of conduct.

Lieutenant Commander Data is a more complex case. In some ways he is the sum of all the identities on the *Enterprise*. Like Wesley, his identity is incomplete and he is always searching to find not just who he is but who he will become. Like Barclay, he struggles with his internal limitations, in Data's case his lack of emotion. Like Picard and Riker, he sometimes loses his identity and has to fight to regain it, frequently becoming a malevolent force like his brother, Lore, or like the cyborg in the *Terminator* movies. But the single most important feature of Data's identity is unquestionably his singularity. He is a completely unique being, one of a kind. *Star Trek* very frequently uses Lieutenant Commander Data to sound the entire register of its concerns with identity. Every feature of identity we have seen in the series occurs with heightened intensity in the case of Data. He is the solitary individual, existing by definition in a state of isolation from the rest of the crew. He has no family and yet is plagued by an evil twin. He is totally devoted to his career as a Starfleet officer and is able to work both day and night. And he is social to the core: although he can exist physically in solitude, he does so only in a state of stasis. There are very few scenes showing Data by himself. All alone he is nothing more than a robot; his various solitary attempts at art, his paintings and poems, are mechanical in the extreme. Data exists only as a mimic, and he is wonderfully played by Brent Spiner, who excels at mimicry and lends to the role an implacable comic calm reminiscent of Buster Keaton. As a mimic, Data comes alive only when in the company of others. He comes alive only when interacting with others, questioning them, learning from them, forming friendships with them.

Data is also the focal point for what we have seen is a central idea of the series: the necessity for society. Again and again we have seen that *Star Trek* views man as the ultimate social creature, thriving in groups but utterly unable to exist alone or in isolation. Isolation in *Star Trek* is always the breeding ground of delusion, madness, or megalomania. All the mad scientists in the series hatch their schemes in lonely corners of the galaxy. The terrible Khan begins his reign of terror during a long exile on a desolate planet. Untrustworthy characters are always renegades, pirates, or individual operatives; members of established societies such as the Klingons or Romulans are generally honorable, or at the very least, concerned with maintaining the appearance of honor. In many ways Data brings us back to Mary Shelley's *Frankenstein,* where, as we have seen, the series often finds its beginnings. Recall that *Frankenstein* is a novel about a monster destroyed by his inability to enter society. The monster comes to self-awareness by concealing himself and observing the movements of a family, but when he exposes himself to them he is driven away, expelled from his birthplace, and hounded to the brink of destruction. In Shelley's novel Dr. Frankenstein's monster can never reenter society, but in *Star Trek* entering human society and becoming a part of it is the sum and substance of the many fables of identity in the series. Data's story, so like that of Frankenstein's monster, may have a better ending, but it has the same premise: that all life is social and conforms to social patterns. The core mission of the *Enterprise* is always to find other life-forms and understand them in their social context, and no missions turn out to be sadder than those where the *Enterprise* confronts beings who are the last of their kind, or beings separated from the social ground that gives them life. Seen in this light, the basic plot of *Star Trek: Voyager,* in which the ship is making its way home across the galaxy, offers something like a skeleton plot seen throughout the series: separation followed by the long journey home.

The plot of separation from society can often be physical, as in the case of *Star Trek: Voyager,* but in this chapter we have seen that it can be psychological as well. Characters in *Star Trek* are often separated from society through the loss of identity, and like the crew of the *Voyager,* they have to make their way home again. As we have seen, this loss can happen in a variety of ways, through isolation, doubling, imprisonment, and torture, to name a few. But the experience of loss almost always turns out to be a strengthening factor in the development of the character. The loss leads to a gain; identity has to be lost in order to be found again. Throughout the series identity develops in what anthropologists call a "liminal" fashion. The basic idea of liminal development is that one has to experience life *outside* society in order to be able to live an adjusted life within society. Most societies have rituals or obligations forcing people to live for a time outside the limits of their normal lives, rituals such as religious retreats and obligations such as military service. They are forced to live life at the margins: thus "liminal," which comes from a Latin word meaning "margins." The liminal journey of the self can be physical, as when Riker is spirited away to a insane asylum (in "Frame of Mind," analyzed in the next chapter), or spiritual, as when Spock submits himself to a Vulcan spiritual discipline. After a time they return to society with a greater sense of direction and purpose. The implication is that social integration requires a degree of built-in disintegration to remain functioning. *Star Trek* offers us a vision of a very well-functioning future, and part of this vision is that, even in a fairly ideal society such as that proposed by the Federation, the experience of liminality must be provided for. It is no accident that, in the final episode of the series, "All Good Things," very few of the *Enterprise* crew are still exploring space. They have taken their places on earth, Picard as a retired ambassador, Data as a distinguished professor at Cambridge, Geordi as a famous novelist. Their voyages around the galaxy ultimately lead them back home, to a higher and more complete sense of identity upon their return. The liminal plot of identity always requires severance and leads to reintegration.

These stories about severance leading to reintegration can often seem far-fetched, because, as we know, severance does not always lead to reintegration. Not everyone who undergoes this kind of separation can be returned to society. There are no deranged war veterans in the series, no former POWs haunted by memories of their captors. Even the malcontents from the Marquis ship on *Star Trek: Voyager,* who are rebels against the Federation and its way of life, successfully adopt Starfleet customs and learn to fit in. In *Star Trek* recovery from loss of identity is often mandated by the structure of the story itself. The liminal movement from severance to reintegration is, after all, a very traditional plot in Western literature, to be found in sources from Homer to Hemingway. In real life Captain Picard could never recover so quickly from his torture from the Borg, and Commander Riker might not recover at all from his abduction by the Tilonians. But in *Star Trek* the structure of the story demands that they recover and be reintegrated, and so they do, usually in the final minutes of the episode, realism be damned. Everyone and everything miraculously returns to normal. In this way the characters of *Star Trek* can often take on a mythic stature, struck down in battle but rising again and again to meet the challenge of the next episode. Despite its relative complexity of character, *Star Trek* is nothing if not faithful to some of the most basic structures of story in our Western tradition. The story of severance and reintegration is one of many recurring stories in *Star Trek,* a root story the series needs to tell not because it is realistic but because it affirms some of our most basic values. The structure of the stories told in the series, their tendency toward myth and the core values they ultimately affirm, will be the subject of the next chapter.

Chapter Three

STORY
and
MYTH

Star Trek has more than one story to tell. Most science fictions are epics, and epics usually tell one extended story. These epics are often wide in scope and cover vast reaches of time and space. The *Dune* novels tell the story of a messiah coming to the planet Dune. The *Foundation* novels of Isaac Asimov tell a single story that takes thousands of years to unfold. The *Star Wars* movies tell the story of the ultimate showdown between the Force and the Evil Empire. Other science fictions have few stories and a large cast of characters. *Star Trek* has a small cast of characters and many, many stories to tell.

The range of the series is remarkable. More than any other science fiction, *Star Trek* ransacks the entire tradition of Western storytelling. Each episode has a tight narrative framed by the captain's log entries. The commercials interrupting the action divide it into five parts, the classic five-act structure of Western drama. Television serials are a fairly recent development, but serialization in literature is not. Serial stories have been told since antiquity, and *Star Trek* masters the serial form in a way that few other shows on television ever have. The series relies on a web of reference to its previous stories to tell new stories every week. One of the hallmarks of literature is this ongoing reference to other stories, especially literary ones. The series has a string of literary borrowings you might expect from T. S. Eliot's *The Waste Land,* not from a television show. Shakespeare is everywhere in *Star Trek,* not only as lifted language but as plot and character, especially the focus Patrick Stewart, an experienced Shakespearean actor, brings to the role of Jean-Luc Picard. There are episodes revolving around the Sherlock Holmes stories, the story of Ahab, the *Beowulf* and *Gilgamesh* epics, and the Homeric hymns. Entire plaents are frequently placed in the position of the Hebrew peoples in the Bible. Cultural memory is one of the great themes of *Star Trek,* especially its transmission through story. In one episode Picard confronts a race that speaks exclusively in metaphorical allusions to certain key myths, much as the Greeks did in using Homer to talk about everything in their society. In another Worf takes a group of Klingon children and teaches them the stories that form the shared basis of their culture, stories that they are in danger of forgetting. No other television show has ever shown this kind of literary range.

But the genuis of *Star Trek* is not simply that it refers to a lot of other stories. It is not the range but the emphasis of these stories that matters. Science fiction is an unusually loose literary genre, and such rampant borrowings are common within it. What matters here is the particular associations that such borrowed stories take on in the series. Uniformly, story in *Star Trek* is a trap, a deception, a trick, or a fraud. On the holodeck stories can be addictive, as Lieutenant Barclay finds out to his chagrin. They can come to life in unexpected ways and try to escape from the holodeck, as Data's Professor James Moriarty does. At times they can even take on a greater force than truth itself, as in the sequence of stories told about the return of a fraudulent messiah, Kahless, to the Klingon Empire. The message *Star Trek* sends about story is clear and consistent. Stories are dangerous. They can get out of control. They have a life of their own and they must be allowed to run their course. Indeed, as we shall see, one of the most common plots in the series shows the crew of the *Enterprise* trapped in a story not of their own making, stories from which they have to escape or suffer confinement, madness, or death. Often stories are such snares that the crew can even get trapped in one of their own. All the episodes about the *Enterprise* being caught in time loops, temporal anomolies in which the crew is made to experience the same story over and over again, essentially explore and amplify this connection between story and entrapment.

This problem may seem surprising, because none of the major characters in *The Next Generation* are particularly adept storytellers. Picard is too private for storytelling, save for the occasional anecdotes about his Academy days. Worf feels alienated from his own Klingon tradition and often tries to pack his son Alexander off to Klingon school; he often complains of having lost his faith in the Klingon tradition. Riker's masculine demeanor can often lend him the bearing of the old figure of the boastful soldier, but he usually refrains from boasting of his sexual conquests, though there is a hint of this in his persistence in asking Captain Picard for tall tales about his younger days. Dr. Crusher is notably reticent about her late husband and her early years, and Deanna Troi has a tendency to interrupt patients' stories in her office, interpreting the stories before the patients are finished telling them. Data is the worst storyteller of all. His poetry is rhythmic to the point of being mechanical, and his narration of events is usually flat and uninspiring. Data is always missing the point of the stories others tell. He never gets jokes and always has to have the punch line explained to him, culminating in a memorable moment in "The Outrageous Okona" when the comic Joe Piscopo appears to teach him how to get laughs. In very many ways, looking over their individual relation to story, the main characters of the series would all seem to inhabit a rational and empirical world in which the capacity for story is no longer important and has begun to atrophy.

Picard, of course, is a narrator of sorts. His voice-over narration framing each episode is a model of truth. The series is full of characters who lie, but not once does the captain of the *Enterprise* make an inaccurate log entry. The log entry establishes a criterion of truth at the beginning of each and every episode. Here, the voice-over seems to say, is a neutral and impartial voice. Here is a trustworthy narrator. Here is a voice which will never deceive you. Picard's voice-over is often the only story in the series that can be trusted, but even this cannot be trusted fully. The three things given in every captain's log are time, date, and place. These have the effect of fixing the *Enterprise* in space and time, and yet, as even the casual viewer knows, the typical *Star Trek* plot has precisely the opposite effect, the effect of unfixing the ship in space and time. Almost every episode of *Star Trek* involves some weird disruption of space or time. The many stories of time travel and sudden transport through space in the series have the cumulative effect of making the certainties of space and time, certainties articulated so serenely in the captain's log, seem positively arbitrary.

And yet, despite the dangers and deceptions they offer, it would seem that stories are somehow essential to space exploration as the series conceives of it. *Star Trek* does more than ransack the Western literary tradition for good stories. The series actively builds them into the hull of the ship. In *The Next Generation* there is a remarkable technology called the holodeck. The holodeck is a device capable of simulating any scene or person in the galaxy. The scenes it summons up are not static, such as landscapes or other beautiful places. More than anything else, the holodeck is a device for summoning up stories. Story is a necessary recreation aboard the *Enterprise,* and the members of the crew pick and choose their favorites from the tradition. The device allows the crew to insert themselves into whatever story they choose. Picard favors detective stories drawn from the novels of Dashiell Hammett. Data likes Sherlock Holmes. Captain Kathryn Janeway of the *Voyager* prefers gothic romance. The perception behind the need for the holodeck is simple: the farther human beings voyage out into the universe, the more they need to remind themselves of the stories telling them who they are. On the *Enterprise* stories are more than recreation. They are part of the basic equipment of the ship, allowing the crew to participate in revitalizing exercises of self-recognition through storytelling. The root meaning of "recognition" is a reknowing or a retelling. The farther the *Enterprise* strays from home, the more its crew actually needs a technology like the holodeck. This can be seen very clearly in the newest series, *Star Trek: Voyager,* where the ship is lost in uncharted space and the holodeck plays a role in nearly every episode. To maintain their sanity, the crew members of the *Voyager* need to keep on making contact with the stories most fundamental to their culture.

The necessity of story is one of the great themes of *Star Trek,* but it always remains a theme fraught with qualification. The power of story to deceive is made manifest in almost every episode in the series, but relatively few stories from the series stress the power of story to communicate the truth. Great storytellers in *Star Trek* are usually deceptive or self-deceived. Story may not be able to speak the plain truth, but the lure of story throughout the series is that story can often speak a higher truth. In *Star Trek* it is when story slides into myth that stories become something other than deceptions. The series of episodes showing Lieutenant Worf's rediscovery of Klingon mythology are a case in point, where it is precisely the fictional character of the myths surrounding Kahless that allows the stories to articulate the essence of the Klingon identity. An even clearer case comes in "Darmok," where we see an entire culture depending on stories for its very language. Story may be necessary, and story may be necessarily deceptive, but story always remains central to *Star Trek* because the series sees stories as the basis for myths, and myths as the basic carriers of cultural identity. "These are our stories," Lieutenant Worf tells a group of Klingon children in "Birthright" after relating to them one of the mythic exploits of Kahless. "They tell us who we are." Story may be misleading, but myth is not. The sum and substance of a culture in *Star Trek* is not reflected in its ships or buildings, distinctive as they may be. The essence of a culture is encapsulated only in its basic stories and fundamental myths, which is why, after all is said and done, the series is willing again and again to tolerate truth in the guise of fiction.

1

The starship *Enterprise* has some very revealing design flaws. The ship may be a technological wonder, but it has two mechanisms aboard that seem especially prone to failure. These mechanisms are the transporter and the holodeck. Transporter malfunctions generally result in threats to character and identity of the sort seen in the last chapter; the doubles of Kirk and Riker were both created by the transporter. Holodeck malfunctions generally result in a completely different domain of problems. The function of the transporter is to move people and things on and off the ship, and when it breaks down, it usually brings an external threat to bear on the *Enterprise,* often a threat of alien origin. The function of the holodeck is to provide illusions for the crew, and when it breaks down, the threat often takes the form of an illusion. The holodeck is the *Enterprise*'s hall of mirrors, a place where the borders between fiction and reality are shifting and uncertain. It is a place of near-perfect illusions, where stories become something more than stories, where fiction is often more of a temptation than a recreation.

The holodeck is often a sleazy place. It is frequently used by crew members to summon up some scenes that would not be out of place in a red-light district. In the holodeck there is an endless procession of bars, nightclubs, pool halls, and even brothels and pleasure planets. In "A Fistful of Datas" the central scene is a bar in an Old West saloon. In "The Outrageous Okona" Data winds up in a comedy club where a group of tables are gathered around a small stage. In *Star Trek: Voyager* the crew often gather for amusement in a sort of French pool hall, a place where there always seem to be a lot of loose women hanging around. In *Deep Space Nine* there is even a repeated implication that Quark rents his holosuites for pornographic purposes. But, true to the places it represents, the holodeck turns out to offer something more than recreation. Sometimes its safety mechanism fails and crew members find themselves in an actual bar or bordello. At other times the threat is more subtle, as when Lieutenant Barclay finds that he prefers the fantasies of the holodeck to his actual life on board the ship. At still other times the holodeck manages to go even farther, effectively blurring the line between illusion and reality, making it difficult to tell what is truth and what is fiction.

The pleasures and pitfalls of the holodeck appear with special vibrancy in an episode called "Hollow Pursuits." The episode begins by showing the normally neurotic Lieutenant Reginald Barclay acting with uncharacteristic confidence in the *Enterprise*'s Ten Forward Bar, which, instead of a lounge, has the feel of a low-life bar. Barclay insults Guinan, is subordinate to La Forge, and wrestles Will Riker to the ground. Only when this little vignette is interrupted by Geordi's voice, ordering Barclay to cargo bay five, do we realize that this is a holodeck simulation. Barclay wearily reports to the cargo bay, where he goes back to being himself again: shy, retiring, and unhappy.

The situation is thus set for a conflict between Barclay's fantasy life and his real life. His fantasy life takes the form of an extended story Barclay tells himself about himself. On the holodeck he appears as a blend of heroic characters, walking with John Wayne swagger and wielding a sword like one of the Three Musketeers. His real life grows less and less real as the episode progresses. Every time something goes wrong in engineering, Barclay returns to the holodeck to seek refuge in his fantasy world. Soon this world becomes less of a recreation and more of an addiction.

The subplot in the episode also underscores how serious this addiction has become. The *Enterprise* is carrying a load of tissue samples to help fight an outbreak of Correllium fever on Nahmi Four. But the medical-sample containers holding the tissue begin to break down. What has happened is that the border insulating a plague bacillus from the ship is not working. In the same way Barclay is not able to separate his fantasy world, supposedly contained in the holodeck, from the rest of the ship. By parallel, the subplot associates the stories Barclay makes up for himself with plague, death, and devastation. As if to clinch the parallel, it is only when he solves the problem of the flawed medical containers, securing the barrier between the plague and the ship, that he is able to become confident enough to secure the barrier between his fantasy life and his real one. The clear implication of the episode is that the stories he is telling himself are a kind of plague, which, if he is not careful, will overtake him and overrun the rest of the ship. The episode ends with Barclay on the holodeck, ending the illusions and erasing the stories. Barclay manages to get rid of most of the programs, but the power of story, and the potential for holodeck addiction, still remains. Even Geordi, who once fell in love with a holodeck illusion himself (in the aptly named episode "Booby Trap") and had to wean himself from it, is sympathetic. "You're gonna be able to write the book on holodiction," he tells him, using the wonderful term in the series for holodeck addiction, which is an appropriate contraction of the words "holodeck," "addiction," and tellingly, "diction," implying that it is the very tendency to speak that gets them into trouble in the first place.

But the power of story, though it has the potential for addiction, is also a necessary and useful power. Throughout the episode Guinan tries to convince Geordi that Lieutenant Barclay has one redeeming feature that is immensely relevant to running a starship: imagination. The word occurs again and again in descriptions of Barclay in all five acts. Of course his imagination has a very evident downside, seen clearly enough in his plague of holodeck fantasies. But in "Hollow Pursuits" it is precisely Barclay's imagination that saves the ship. By act five, the ship is shaking hard and the destruction of the *Enterprise* is imminent. At the last moment Barclay, and Barclay alone, figures out that an element called invidium, used in medical containment fields, is causing the problem with the warp engines, and the ship is saved. The crew gather around Barclay and congratulate him after his saving idea. "Glad you were with us out here in the real world today, Mr. Barclay," Geordi tells him. But the truth is that Barclay saves the ship because he is partly *not* in the real world, because he draws his energy and imagination from a fantasy life to which, if he is not careful, he can become addicted. Story thus cuts both ways in this episode. Barclay realizes that he needs to preserve the capacity for story, which is why he does not erase all of his programs in the very last scene of the episode. But he also needs to keep stories in check, preventing them from overrunning the ship like a plague and turning him into a hapless addict.

The specific idea of holodeck addiction appears in a number of other episodes, but the theme of story as a threatening addiction runs throughout the series. Another example is "The Game." Here the story is not much of a story but a seemingly simple game. The player puts on a visor and sees images of a playing field. A series of small circles float above the field, and the player has to grasp the circles and pull them down to the field. The game seems harmless enough, but think again. It rewards a successful action by stimulating the pleasure center of the brain. It violates *Star Trek*'s usual taboo about crossing the line between the body and machine (seen with greatest clarity, as shown in the first chapter, in the case of the Borg). And it lures the player into a simple and repetitive action that must be performed over and over again. The implication here is that simple and repetitive stories are the most dangerous of all. Certain kinds of highly addictive kinds of stories such as romance novels or pornography follow this same exact pattern, using alluring and repetitive images to perform the same sequence of actions over and over again. In this episode the repeated story is reduced to its bare bones, but the resolution of the quandry is still relatively simple. All you have to do is take the visor off and stop playing the game, which is finally what the crew does.

A greater danger to the ship is posed when stories try to escape their ordinary settings. The idea of a story attempting to become something more than a story, to become real, is the subject of an episode called "Ship in a Bottle." The episode begins with Data on the holodeck running one of his Sherlock Holmes programs. A Sherlock Holmes story is a highly structured kind of mystery story with very set characters and plot. Data runs the program because he can face a restricted problem in a restricted setting, but in this case the problem and the setting get out of control. Sherlock Holmes's nemesis, Professor James Moriarty, a character saved and stored in the program from a previous episode ("Elementary, Dear Data"), appears and asks to see Captain Picard. As a character in a holodeck program, Moriarty should not be aware that he is not real, but apparently he is. He says he was created too well: "I became self-aware; I am alive." In the next few moments Moriarty relates his sufferings as a self-aware fictional character. It is an extraordinary account. Saved in the memory banks of the computer, Moriarty was aware of the passage of time. He experienced "brief, terrifying periods of consciousness, disembodied, without substance." This is a remarkable testimony to the power of human beings to breathe life into their stories. Here is a character so real that even he has begun to believe in his own reality. Throughout the episode, of course, it turns out that Professor Moriarty is not real and never was. He has only managed to convince the crew of the *Enterprise* that he is real by simulating the entire ship within the holodeck and running them, in effect, through an elaborate stage. But the confusion about where fiction ends and reality begins is very real. Throughout "Ship in a Bottle" the border of story shifts from act to act. In one act we think that Moriarty and his story have crossed over into the *Enterprise;* in the next we see that Moriarty has lured the crew into his story simulation of their world; in the last we see crew managing to convince Moriarty that his existence on the holodeck really is real. The episode ends with a restoration of the real, with Moriarty repatriated to the holodeck and Picard and the crew back on the ship, but the crew members have clearly been shaken by their experience with story. Though Moriarty was an illusion, for a time he was all too real.

So in "Ship in a Bottle," as in the other holodeck episodes, the holodeck finally poses only a limited threat to truth. The holodeck episodes all end with the restoration of reality. Each episode opens and then shuts the book of fiction. The endings of holodeck episodes all show fictional characters returning to their place in a computer program; they are often shown disappearing like the illusions they are. Even Professor Moriarty is shown, in the end, to be an illusion drifting within his world of illusion. But at the end of "Ship in a Bottle" Picard asks a revealing question. Gesturing around him in the observation lounge, Picard asks, "Might all this be nothing more than an elaborate simulation being run inside a little device, sitting on someone else's table?" The question is more than rhetorical. As we shall see, in a great many episodes *Star Trek* actually poses the problem in a serious, if slightly different form. What if we are really only part of a story? What if that story controls us instead of us controlling it? What if story is a kind of prison?

2

Story in *Star Trek* is sometimes a literal prison, with walls and a door, a place to which there is entrance but no exit. We have already seen Professor Moriarty complain of his sense of confinement in a holodeck story, but the confining power of story is not restricted to the holodeck. Stories tend to get told over and over again, and the sense of structure and repetition so crucial to the telling of any story frequently leads the series to associate stories with circularity, confusion, and repetition. The crew of the *Enterprise* are often made to experience events over and over again in the simple form of a time loop. Other experiences of story repetition are more complex, and the crew often have to wrench themselves free from a story not of their own making. Still other experiences are so uncannily complicated that it is very difficult to tell where the story is coming from, who is telling it, and even whether it is a story at all. In each of these cases the crew of the *Enterprise* must break free of the directing power of story. In the best sense, as we shall see, story can shade into myth and carry with it the force of religious revelation. At its worst, story is a form of imprisonment leading to isolation and madness. The regular implication throughout the series is that story, though it can sometimes be liberating, can also be a trap, a direct infringement upon the human freedom which the series values so highly.

The simplest form of the story trap is the time loop episode, of which many examples appear in the series. "Cause and Effect" is generally acknowledged to be the best of these. The episode has far and away the most enticing teaser of the entire series. In the first minute of the teaser an optical shows the *Enterprise* exploding in a firestorm of debris. The ship has been completely destroyed.

The next thing we see is the ship cruising along at impulse as if nothing had happened. Riker, Data, Worf, and Beverly are playing five-card stud in Riker's quarters. The game is interrupted when Dr. Crusher is summoned to sickbay. Crusher is struck by a sudden feeling that she has done this before, a feeling of déjà vu. The scene then cuts to the next day, when we see a starship emerging from the murky area in space. The ship is clearly on a collision course with the *Enterprise*. The other ship collides with the *Enterprise*'s starboard nacelle, putting it into a spin. Now everything happens just as it did in the teaser. Again the ship explodes, and again the *Enterprise* is completely destroyed.

The same story is slated to happen four more times in the course of this episode. The first time it appears basically without variation, and this is the hardest rerun of the story to watch. The crew members are caught in a story without knowing it, disturbed only by a slight peripheral awareness that they have done all of this before. Again we see the emergence of the other ship, the crash, the flaring, the final destruction. Then, after the commercial break, the story returns to square one and begins all over again. The story starts to happen in exactly the same order, but with one crucial difference. Members of the crew now begin to realize that they have experienced this story before. At the poker game the players now can predict the exact progression of the cards being dealt. By the time the distortion appears and the ship explodes, nearly everyone on board has experienced a feeling that they have all done this before.

The *Enterprise* is saved when the crew breaks the cycle of repetition and reenters linear time. Breaking the cycle involves becoming aware that stories, far from being perfectly circular, are slightly different every time. It is through a minute awareness of the slight deviations from story to story that the crew members learn how to save themselves from the impending crash. The minute they begin to deviate from the pattern of the story, they are free from the imprisoning force of the story. The way they deviate from the pattern of the story is by becoming aware of it, and the entire episode chronicles a coming-to-awareness of the power of story. The story repeats a total of six times, and only as soon as they are aware of its basic patterns of repetition can they break free of it. The crew members send themselves a message from one story to the next, thus breaking free from the story cycles. In the last telling of the story it begins to change in the telling, a clear sign that the *Enterprise* is about to burst out of its story trap. The cards dealt in the poker game in Riker's quarters are now different. When the other ship appears out of the space-time distortion, Data now knows that his idea of using a tractor beam will not save the ship. He agrees with Riker's suggestion that they decompress a shuttle bay instead. The collision is averted and the ship is saved.

The use of the poker game throughout "Cause and Effect" reinforces the sense of the strictures of story. The deck of cards is a good emblem for the repetitive yet varied nature of storytelling. There are fifty-two different cards in a deck, a small number considering the vastness of different combinations of cards and styles of card playing. The playing of a card game is extremely repetitive, and yet it also has its own form of suspense. That suspense, however, is restricted to the players themselves. No card game has ever become a spectator sport; card games are too repetitive to allow for more than a little variation, and they are not exciting to watch. And yet it is finally through a slight variation in the card game that the crew in "Cause and Effect" learns that it is trapped in a time loop even more confining than a game of cards. An unexpected variation turns up in the card game in Riker's quarters. Instead of the same cards played over and over again—an eight, an ace, a queen, and a four—Data deals out four threes. The cycle of repetition has been broken; they have successfully sent themselves a message from the last story, and that message is simple: *You are caught in a story and must get out.* When they burst out of the time loop, the captain of the other ship comes on the viewscreen. He identifies himself as the captain of the U.S.S. *Bozeman,* a Soyuz-class starship that has not been in service for over eighty years. The *Enterprise* was caught in the time loop for seventeen days, but this ship has been in a loop for eighty years and might have remained there for all time if the *Enterprise* had not come along to burst the bubble of the story.

The theme of the crew caught in a story is explored in even greater depth in an episode called "The Royale." In episodes like "The Game" and "Cause and Effect" the *Enterprise* is caught in a repetitive sequence of actions that barely qualifies for the name of story; the "stories" here are more like the rudimentary and endlessly repeated scenarios of a computer game than like a typical story with plot, character, and a story line. "The Royale" is different. In this episode the crew of the *Enterprise* gets caught in a full-fledged story with a plot and characters, a setting and a style. The story, however, is a bad story. At the end of "Ship in a Bottle" Picard says that Professor Moriarty should be able to spend the rest of his life happily exploring the inner workings of the Sherlock Holmes stories; the sense here is that a good story can be a very satisfying sort of prison and can offer tremendous variation. But a bad story can be a terrifying fate, a place not only of circularity but of caricature, not just a form of prison but a kind of hell.

One such bad story is the basis of "The Royale." The episode begins as the *Enterprise* enters orbit around a planet in the Theta 116 solar system. The surface of the planet is uninhabitable, seared by winds and blasted by lightning and tornadoes. Riker informs Picard that they have detected debris of some sort in loose orbit around the planet. When they beam a section aboard for analysis, they find a piece of jagged metal decorated with a white five-pointed star, the insignia of the United States Air Force. Picard decides to risk a minimal away team, and the team materializes in a dim black void. The place is empty except for an old-fashioned revolving door.

The away team goes through the door and finds itself in the lobby of the Hotel Royale, a Las Vegas-style hotel where there is quite a story in progress, a love triangle involving a bellhop, a gangster, and his moll. Entering one of the rooms, the team members find a skeleton of a human male, long dead, wearing an American astronaut's uniform that identifies him as Colonel S. Richey. On the nightstand next to him are two documents: a novel and a diary with only one entry in it. Riker reads Colonel Richey's diary and learns that an alien presence, who accidentally destroyed Richey's craft, tried to make amends by recreating the world of the novel, which they took to be a guide to human behavior. The novel is called *Hotel Royale,* and its story is conventional in the extreme. The characters are cardboard and act in extremely predictable ways. The gangster kills the bellhop who loves his girl. The aliens who created the Hotel Royale did their best to be faithful to the novel, but the novel was so bad that their only achievement was to have created a fictional hell in which hell is a bad fiction.

But how to get out? Reading through the novel, the members of the away team realize that in order to leave the story they must participate in it. Apparently one of the subplots of *Hotel Royale* involves a trio of foreign investors who show up and break the bank. So Riker, Data, and Worf pose as foreign investors. But now they are part of the story and find themselves carried along by the current of the story. Once Data breaks the bank at the casino tables, they succeed in winning the deed to the hotel itself. The Hotel Royale is now theirs, and they are free to leave it. Unlike the American astronaut, who died alienated from the story, the away team from the *Enterprise* realizes that there is no alternative to telling stories. In the end, the team members have to own the story in order to be free of it, and once they do, they are able to leave the Hotel Royale via the revolving door.

In "The Royale," then, there is no life outside story. The episode uses the vivid image of the revolving door to show that there are not many alternatives to telling stories. On one side of the revolving door is a story. On the other is a featureless black void. The implication is that outside of stories, there is nothing at all, no life, no consciousness, no color, and no variation. In "The Royale" the condition of life itself, even of the foreshortened style of living represented by a gangster existence, is that life seems to require the organization of story. Basic to human existence is the need to consume stories. The benevolent entity that kidnapped the American astronaut seemed to have recognized this, and labored to provide him with a story which, it believed, would provide him with mental sustenance and a familiar environment. The cruel irony of "The Royale" is that the entity based its reconstruction of human stories not on our higher system of myths but on our lower system of stories. A gangster story is told not for edification but for amusement, and is meant to provide temporary diversion from life, not a sustaining examination of it. The benevolent entity was right to see that its human charge required stories to stay alive in outer space, but wrong to assume that the gangster novel was one of these sustaining stories. It also did not know that stories do not exist on their own but are always part of larger systems of stories. When Data plays at being Sherlock Holmes, he does not simply repeat one of Conan Doyle's famous tales. Rather, he programs the computer to recreate the *world* of Sherlock Holmes and provide him with variations on the theme. Colonel Richey, however, is trapped inside a story without variations. His story is slightly larger in scope than the time loop of "Cause and Effect," but it shares the same qualities of circularity and repetition, qualities aptly summed up in the episode's use of the revolving door as the entry point to the story.

In these two episodes, "Cause and Effect" and "The Royale," the worst that can happen is being caught in a story over and over again. Spending an eternity doing the same thing is certainly a kind of hell, and the crew feels pity for the American astronaut who died in this revolving door of a story. But *Star Trek* imagines an even worse fate than mere circularity. There are repetitive stories in *Star Trek* in which the world does not remain the same but grows smaller and smaller with each telling. A story can be a trap, but it can also be a slowly tightening noose.

This sense of story as a slow strangulation appears in one of the most remarkable episodes of the series, "Frame of Mind." The episode begins in an asylum cell where Will Riker is being interviewed by a staff doctor. Riker is trying to please the doctor and say the right thing, playing the part of the cooperative patient. But he is tense and his temper flares. A turn of the camera then reveals that we are in the ship's theater, that the asylum cell is actually a set on a stage. The theater is empty except for Data, who is playing the doctor, and Beverly Crusher, who is directing the play. They decide to call it quits for the day, and Riker confesses to being frustrated with the role.

On opening night Riker delivers an authentic performance, impersonating a madman with great passion. When the play is over, the audience is gone. Riker is now in a prison and there is a cell wall where the audience used to be. In place of the cheering there is silence.

This change in Riker's frame of mind is the first in a rapid succession of many frames of mind throughout the episode. For several acts Riker goes back and forth between the theater and the asylum cell until he becomes uncertain which is which. The asylum cell is on Tilonus Four, where apparently he has been accused of murder and confined to ward forty-seven of the Tilonus Institute for Mental Disorders. A doctor appears and in a calm voice tells Riker that he has been experiencing delusions that he is an officer aboard a starship and that the aim of his treatment in the ward has been to restore his memory. A series of rapid movements between the prison and the stage now follows, which effectively conveys Riker's mounting confusion about who he is and where he has been. The rapid succession of frames of mind is handled wonderfully and with great cinematic precision. The last frame in each of these series always turns out to be the prison cell, and gradually Riker comes to accept the doctor's assertion that he is a murderer who has repressed the memory of his crime. "I need help," Riker tells him. "I don't want to be at the mercy of these hallucinations any more."

Just as Riker is on the brink of believing himself mad, Data and Worf break in and beam him to the *Enterprise.* Examined by Dr. Crusher in sickbay, Riker grabs a phaser and shoots himself with it. The blast has no effect on him, but the entire room shatters like breaking glass, revealing that he is back in his asylum cell. When he fires again, he is back in the theater on the ship. Now Riker looks around him and sees the stage itself. He starts punching holes in it with his fists, and suddenly the scene shatters one last time and he is in the real world. He is lying on an examination table in an alien laboratory, where he has been the whole time. Grabbing his communicator, he calls for an emergency transport and, dematerializing, is returned to the ship, where Picard tells him that he was abducted on Tilonus and injected with drugs to extract strategic information from him. He tells him to get some rest, but Riker says that there is one thing he would like to do first. The final scene shows Riker in the theater of the *Enterprise,* breaking down the stage of the asylum cell.

The episode is a study in the power of theater. A story told in a theater is an amplified and considerably more dangerous form of storytelling. A story in a book can be open and closed at will. But a story in a theater requires impersonation on the part of the actors and entrapment on the part of the audience. In a play an audience must stay in a darkened room until the end of the performance, and the actors must labor at becoming someone else. A performance in the theater thus possesses in heightened form all the dangers already seen by *Star Trek* in storytelling. By definition, a play requires impersonation and entrapment, and all the great playwrights, from Shakespeare to Pirandello, have been aware of the devious nature of theatrical storytelling art. In "Frame of Mind" precisely these twin elements of theatrical power form the basis of Riker's nightmare abduction. Entering the play at the beginning of the episode, he is carried away by the logic of the theater into a world of impersonation and entrapment. As the episode proceeds, Riker becomes less and less sure who he is and more and more trapped. "I can't get it out of my head," he says at one point about the play. The heightened form of story represented by theater draws him in and does not let him go. Riker is trapped within so many layers of stories that he must shatter them all in order to finally go free. Thus the remarkable sequence of scenes in act five, where Riker destroys fiction after fiction thrown at him by his Tilonian captors, revealing them for the fabricated frames of mind that they are. Story after story is shattered, until the last story ends and Riker is returned to the *Enterprise,* where his first action is to restore his own frame of mind by destroying the frame of the story he has just experienced by dismantling the theater set of Beverly Crusher's play.

"Frame of Mind" is the title of Dr. Crusher's play, but the story foisted upon Riker in the episode is of alien fabrication. Escaping from aliens is tantamount to escaping from story and destroying the theater. The disturbing implication here is that although story does seem to be an inescapable part of human existence, we are all somehow alienated from the stories we tell. *Stories are alien.* They have their own existence and it is not the same as ours. The only times Commander Riker is fully himself in "Frame of Mind" is when he manages to step outside the frame of a story. Otherwise he is caught along in the rush of a narrative not of his own making. Stories precede us and they seem to have a life of their own. In "Frame of Mind" the life of stories is more than a surrogate for life; it is a substitute for life. A succession of fictions really can become like alien life-forms, kidnapping us, taking us away from ourselves, transporting us into a different reality, or realities, in which we no longer can tell truth from fiction.

The frame for this succession of fictions is, aptly enough, a play. The episode begins with Riker's hesitation about acting in the play; he is wary of participating in a play, because it means being something other than what he is. But once Riker crosses the line and begins to impersonate someone else, it almost seems as if there is no turning back. Once he crosses the border from reality into fiction, everything becomes fictional. In the world of the play, fiction taints the real; Riker can no longer tell what is part of the play and what is part of the world. This is not simply another case of alien abduction. Riker is not simply spirited away and subjected to interrogation and torture, as Picard was in "Chain of Command." He is abducted and stripped of his ability to tell fiction from reality. The developing menace of "Frame of Mind" is due precisely to a rapid succession of equally plausible fictions. Whenever the scene shifts, Riker is left wondering whether this is real, whether the last scene was real, whether any of it is or was real. Significantly, we lose sight of exactly why he was kidnapped in the first place. It is as if the rapid-fire sequence of fictions has its own momentum and Riker is carried along with it whether he likes it or not. Even when "Frame of Mind" is over, it is unclear what the Tilonians wanted with him. As in "Chain of Command," torture is carried out for its own sake. In "Frame of Mind," however, the aliens seem to have discovered a higher form of torture. Picard is physically tortured. Riker is deprived of his ability to perform one of the most basic operations of human consciousness: telling fiction from reality.

The inability to tell fiction from reality effectively turns every story into a prison. In "Frame of Mind" there are a succession of prison cells, each slightly different, each equally fictional. So prevalent in *Star Trek* is this idea of story as prison that it has the net effect of raising serious and fundamental questions about the nature of story itself. What is it about the telling of stories that leads to circularity, entrapment, and death? There are many stories in our tradition about storytellers using their arts to stay alive; that old story from *The Arabian Nights* tells of Scheherazade telling stories to fend off death; as long as she talks and tells, she stays alive; very few stories show storytelling leading to death. In *Star Trek* Data's evil brother is called Lore, a word that is a synonym for story, and he is a being so dangerous that in one episode, "Descent," Data has to put him to death. Why are stories so dangerous in *Star Trek*?

3

The answer has to do with the proximity of story to myth. In *Star Trek* story is always close to lying, while myth is always close to truth. Episodes exploring the inner structure of a story tend to stress its dangers and pitfalls, while episodes exploring the inner structure of a myth tend to stress its benefits and rewards. "The Royale," as discussed earlier, is a clear case in point. It tells a gangster story with no mythic implications whatsoever, and uniformly, that story is menacing, circular, and imprisoning. Even more, it tells a bad story, and as we all know, bad stories have a tendency to be both circular and formulaic. The crew caught in the story of the Hotel Royale cannot help at times but laugh at its own plight, but the situation in many other stories in many other such episodes is much more serious because the crew members are not aware that they are caught in a story. In "Frame of Mind" Riker loses the capacity to see that he is in a story; in "Cause and Effect" the whole crew loses that capacity and has to struggle to regain it. The only alternative here is to break out of the story and stop telling it. A typical ending to one of these story-as-prison episodes comes in "Frame of Mind." In the last frame of the episode we see Will Riker taking apart the stage that had become the theater of his own mental collapse. The scene makes the connection between story and imprisonment directly and very vividly, for the stage set he is destroying represents a prison cell. To get out of prison, he must destroy the stage and, in effect, stop telling the story.

But not all stories. The *Enterprise* can often get caught in the vicious circle of a story, but not all stories are vicious circles. Certain stories, though quite fictional, evidently have a redeeming potential. In *Star Trek* the closer a story is to a myth, the more it begins to transcend its status as a fiction. Conversely, the closer a myth is to a story, the more it appears fabricated and false. The line between story and myth in *Star Trek* is porous and shifting and is the subject of much confusion. On first contact with a new culture the crew of the *Enterprise* always has to sort out its necessary mythologies from its extraneous stories. This is not always easy to do. Various characters in the series often deceive crew members by offering them a story under the guise of myth, as in "Man of the People," where Ves Alkar has Deanna Troi handle a stone she thinks is part of a ritual of mourning. Story can often masquerade as myth and perform its work of entrapment, and predictably in this episode, Deanna begins to act in exactly the same manner as a previous woman who had also handled the stone, showing once again how easy it is for a story to repeat itself and get mixed up with a myth. Stories are told to amuse, and myths to edify, and yet even in literary history there is a long-standing and unresolved controversy about how to classify them. Story and myth are always shading into one another, and part of the mission of the *Enterprise* is learning to tell them apart.

The gray area between story and myth is the subject of a remarkable series of episodes dealing with Lieutenant Worf's rediscovery of his Klingon identity. "Birthright," a two-part episode in which Worf teaches basic Klingon myths to some refugee Klingon children, tends to look on myths as mere stories, fictions that perform an important social function as the carriers of Klingon cultural identity, but fictions nonetheless, stories that have very little reality value. The situation is far different in "Rightful Heir." In this episode myth assumes a position of importance far beyond that of story. In an episode like "Birthright" myths are by implication stories we tell our children, stories more suited to children than to adults. In "Rightful Heir," however, a character from a myth threatens to undo the very fabric of the Klingon Empire. This episode is about a myth that suddenly comes to life, and it explores what happens when fiction becomes reality and myth enters history.

In "Rightful Heir" Worf tells Captain Picard that his effort to try to teach Klingon children the basic Klingon stories (in "Birthright") led him to realize that his own belief in Kahless, the Klingon messiah, is deficient. Captain Picard now grants Worf an extended period of leave so that he can immerse himself in Klingon beliefs to discover whether they hold any truth for him. The basic plot of the episode is immediately established: Worf has been given leave to come to terms with the power of myth.

Worf now goes by shuttle to the planet Boreth, a planet sacred to all Klingons because there the followers of Kahless await his return, where he takes up residence at a Klingon temple in the mountains. Worf meditates for days, but he does not see Kahless. "I have had no visions, I have received no insight," he tells the head cleric, Koroth. He starts to pack his bag in preparation for returning to the *Enterprise.*

Koroth persuades Worf to give his meditation one more try, and this time Kahless appears. Worf asks the episode's key question about myth when he turns to Kahless and asks, "You are real?" Kahless sidesteps the question with an assertion: "I am Kahless and I have returned."

Worf scans Kahless with his tricorder and is surprised to find that this Kahless is fully Klingon. When Kahless asks Worf whether he believes in him, Worf answers, "I want to believe."

The possibility of that belief becomes more and more elusive as the episode proceeds. The *Enterprise* is now summoned to ferry Kahless back to the Klingon home world.

Kahless starts telling a mythic story, this one about a foolish man who goes outside the walls of a city, tries to fight the wind, and is killed by his folly. There is a reverential silence after Kahless has finished speaking, but then Chancellor Gowron of the Klingon high council asks a question in an insistent voice. "What was his name? If you were really there, you should be able to tell us the name of the man outside the walls." This is a remarkable moment, for here a myth is being interrogated not for its story value but for its reality value. Gowron refuses to take the myth in its own terms. He treats the myth not as a special type of story holding a special kind of meaning but as merely a very old and very questionable form of story. Gowron turns out to be right about Kahless but wrong about the power of myth. Kahless turns out to be a clone created in a laboratory by the high clerics of Boreth, and Gowron manages to defeat him in hand-to-hand combat.

But the myth of Kahless is even more powerful than the reality of the clone. The fiction of Kahless may be a fraud, but the fiction is stronger than the fraud. Gowron confides to Picard that the *idea* of Kahless is stronger than the man: "Have you ever fought an *idea*, Picard? It has no weapon to destroy, no body to kill." The disembodied idea of Kahless is the myth of Kahless, the weave of many stories passed down for generations among the Klingons. Gowron can discredit Kahless the clone, but there is no discrediting Kahless the myth. Already word of Kahless's return has spread throughout the Klingon Empire, and a group of Klingons have started to worship Kahless aboard the *Enterprise.* Their faith is clearly unaffected by his evident fictional status. Because civil war is brewing, Worf now offers a compromise. If Kahless will admit that he is clone, he can assume a ceremonial function as Klingon emperor, while Chancellor Gowron can still hold the reins of power. The compromise proves acceptable, and the Klingon Empire is safe for the moment, turning from the fear of dissolution to the hope of renewal.

The myth of Kahless would seem to promise renewal, and yet such myths of renewal are often deceptive signs of decline. Throughout *Star Trek* the Klingon Empire is poised on the edge of a desperate decline. The Empire made peace with the Federation in *Star Trek VI: The Undiscovered Country* because it came very close to destroying itself by mismanaging its own natural resources. Every episode of the series shows the Klingon Empire to be on the brink of collapse and civil war. Koroth, the high cleric in "Rightful Heir," fears that his people will go on sacrificing their honor until "they are no different from Romulans." In the *Star Trek* universe the

Klingons seem to be a society on the decline. Their recourse to myth, that is, their revival of an old myth, is often a symptom of mass hysteria among societies that have lost their sense of direction and base of power. In the 1890s a new wave of myths called the "ghost dances" swept the Plains Indians of the United States. These myths seemed to promise that the tribes, so decimated by the white settlers, would again regain their old prominence throughout the land. But the revived myth was merely a consolation, a collective deception at a moment of great despair. In the *Star Trek* universe the Klingons seem to have arrived at such a moment in "Rightful Heir." By the end of this episode, they have become so despairing of their rightful place in the galaxy that they are even willing to allow a laboratory clone to symbolically rule over them. What appears to be a sign of a revived Klingon Empire may be, in this broader view, another step along a long slow road of decline. Kahless is their last hope; the spiritual state of crisis of the Klingons is the result of the political state of crisis in the Klingon Empire (empires often shift religious allegiances in their final moments, as in the case of the Romans turning to Christianity). Societies reviving myths in *Star Trek* are always shown getting into trouble, as in "Devil's Due," where an old myth of a returning devil has to be discredited by the crew of the *Enterprise.* The universe is thus left open to the Federation, which seems to specialize not in inflating old myths but in exploding them.

But myth has its own attendant rewards. If in *Star Trek* story is always trying to pull the *Enterprise* into a world of story, myth is always trying to pull the ship into a world of myth. The stories tend to be traps, but the myths tend to be mazes. Stories typically appear associated with time loops, prisons, and other images of circularity and confinement. In myth, circularity is much more likely to be liberating: the way out, not the way in. In *Star Trek*'s mythical tales the crew must join the story rather than escape from it. The problem in these episodes thus becomes not escaping the story but trying to understand the story in its own terms. This is often hard to do, because in myth the story line is often clouded by a haze of symbolism. The bad stories in which the *Enterprise* is caught in "The Royale" have few symbolic overtones, but the myths it encounters are full of symbols that require sustained acts of interpretation. In this series stories are traps that need to be escaped, while myths are openings that need to be interpreted. In "Rightful Heir" Worf correctly interprets the reappearance of Kahless as an opportunity to attempt to unify the Klingon Empire. Even though the story of Kahless is, strictly speaking, untrue, the myth of Kahless is not. Myths must be approached on their own terms, or not at all.

The approach to myth on its own terms is exactly the subject of one of the later episodes of *The Next Generation,* "Masks." In this episode the *Enterprise* encounters a rouge comet in Sector 1156, a large chunk of material surrounded by a haze of ice that has been en route for eighty-seven million years. For a moment the lights on the bridge of the *Enterprise* flare brightly. Apparently, the *Enterprise* is being scanned. Reports come in from various decks on the ship; various artifacts, small statues and columns, have begun to appear all over the ship. Among the objects are a variety of masks inscribed with alien ideographic symbols. To find out what is happening, the *Enterprise* fires its phasers to melt away the outer shell of the comet. The steaming mass of the comet in "Masks" conceals a huge Mayan-looking piece of technology decorated with the same masks and icons that have been appearing all over the ship.

This device is an archive. Space in *Star Trek* is full of archives. These are usually last recordings of long-vanished civilizations. They are not passive records, message in high-tech bottles. Rather they are probes, intrusive and penetrating, carriers of the memory of dead civilizations. In *Star Trek* the galaxy seems to have as many dead civilizations as live ones. In some ways the galaxy in *Star Trek* is much more like Europe, a place of many dead and vanished cultures, than like America, where large-scale human activity is a more recent phenomenon. Despite the injunction of the series "to boldly go where no one has gone before," most of space is full of cultures that have been there before. In a way it is a shame that *Star Trek* changed "where no man has gone before" in the original series to "where no one has gone before." Seen within the series, the original wording is, in fact, far more accurate. The *Enterprise* is constantly going where no *man* has been before, but not where no one has been. Many, many beings have been where the *Enterprise* has been; it is simply that human beings have not been there before. The presence of so many archives in space is voluble testimony to *Star Trek*'s essentially historical view of mythology. Myths are not eternal; they live and die in rhythm with the societies that have created them. Archives that attempt to foist old mythologies on new societies must be fought off; the old myths, like the old gods in the original *Star Trek*'s classic episode "Who Mourns for Adonis?", must be laid to rest.

The resurgent myths in "Masks" soon begin to pose a threat to the ship. Alien symbols start floating around inside the ship's computer, symbols dominated by a stylized image of the sun. Other symbols now appear, symbols that Data interprets as being symbols for "boundary," "border," "road," "companion," "message," "messenger," and "death." He immediately assumes that these symbols are not random but are part of a mythical system organized in a particular story line. The problem is, the crew of the *Enterprise* does not know what those stories are.

The rest of the episode is occupied with the trying to find out the story upon which the mythical symbols are based. The symbols themselves have no meaning without the crew knowing how they are organized in a story. Today's archaeologists are often capable of deciphering languages, but they are not often capable of interpreting them because they are not familiar with the mythical stories to which those languages often referred. When Michael Ventris deciphered the ancient dialect of Minoan Crete, Linear-B, in 1952, the discovery was hailed as the key to the language. But it was not. Much of the language remains unintelligible because, even once translated, it is full of proper names and other references to long-forgotten myths. A myth is, after all, a story told about events of divine origin. Without knowing the story, the myth becomes unintelligible, and the language based upon those myths remains a mystery, even though the grammar is known.

In "Masks," then, the crew of the *Enterprise* must decipher the grammar of story underlying the myths now appearing throughout the ship. This is not easy to do. The archive transforms Data into a kind of John the Baptist figure named Ihat, who warns of the imminent appearance of a god named Masaka. Picard pleads with Data to speak with Masaka, but Data (still Ihat) keeps insisting that "Only Korgano can talk to Masaka." Finally Ihat tells Picard that in order to confront Masaka, he must build a temple for the god to appear in. The holodeck quickly provides Picard with such a temple, but like a translator of ancient language, Picard still does not know what to do with the temple. He still does not know the story, but now he sets himself to interpreting the symbols and placing them together in some kind of cogent narrative. The "sun," the "moon," a "death" . . . Picard soon realizes that the symbols refer to the setting of the sun and the rising of the moon. Masaka is the sun god and Korgano is the moon god who supplants her every night. So Picard takes a mask of Korgano, the moon god, and enters the temple of the sun god, Masaka. Entering the myth and playing the role of Korgano, he tells Masaka that it is time to sleep so as to awake again at dawn. Only when Masaka relinquishes her power to Korgano does control of the *Enterprise* return to Picard. Data returns to normal; the artifacts disappear from the ship; and in the last scene we see Data in the art studio, sculpting a replica of one of the alien masks.

The style of the masks seen throughout the ship gives the mythic world a very particular inflection. The script of the episode calls for the mask to be "a kind of cross between the Venetian and the Mayan," and the mask itself is beautifully executed blend of the two, a sort of opera mask with chiseled stone features. The decision to blend these particular two styles is quite revealing. The mythical society confronted by the *Enterprise* in "Masks" wears two different masks. The Mayan mask evokes the culture of ancient Mexico. This mask is primitive and ritualistic in the extreme, worshipping the movements of a particular sun and moon that can only seem arbitrary, given the comet's long journey across outer space. The Venetian mask evokes the culture of Venice, a city of explorers and merchants that created a far-flung empire in the fourteenth century. The mask, in other words, shows the world of myth in two aspects. The first is inward-directed and grounded in an agrarian culture, very much the typical world we associate with societies based on mythic systems. The second aspect, the Venetian, is more disturbing. It shows that an outward-directed, urban, sophisticated society can still rely on mythic forms and be based on a mythic understanding of reality. The Masakan society is fully primitive and fully technological at the same time. It brings up a fear regarding human progress often seen elsewhere in *Star Trek*. What if human beings are not evolving toward a perfectly rational, perfectly technological society? What if the ultimate end of technological development is a return to myth?

Much science fiction is preoccupied with this idea, and *Star Trek* has its own twist on it. Systems of myths generally evolve in technically deficient societies as explanations for forces of nature that those societies do not possess the means to understand. Science fiction is often set in a time, past or future, when human beings are bent on exploring a largely unknown universe. This confrontation with the unknown recapitulates early experience with the unknown forces of nature, and these forces often elicit a mythic response. Myths in *Star Trek* constantly come up in connection with incomplete stories, insoluble mysteries, and puzzles. The archive in "Masks" is one such mystery. We never find out who created it, when, or why. But the mystery itself is immediately invested in mythic terms. Moments of first contact, as I will show later in this chapter, tend overwhelmingly to be crystallized in mythic terms. At its most basic, myth offer a familiar vocabulary for dealing with the unknown. Lieutenant Worf may not believe in the Klingon afterlife, Sto-Vo-Kor, but the myth provides him with a way of containing the mystery in language. Myth is a way of making the mysteries of the universe manageable by placing them in that most human of all things: language. The return to myth can be threatening, as in "Masks," where monuments threaten to crush the ship, but seen in its own terms, myth can also offer a viable system of explanation for the world and the way it works. The lesson of "Masks" is that no myth is nonsense. Picard can and does figure it out, seeing how the sun and moon have accurate positions within the Masakan mythical system, and the ship is saved.

In "Masks," then, acknowledging the power of myth is what saves the ship. It is only when Picard realizes that Masaka is a sun god who needs to be cajoled into setting that he is able to get her to abdicate her power over the ship. To do this, Picard must participate voluntarily in the myth itself. He puts on the ceremonial mask of the myth so he will be able to take it off again. He must enter the mythical world to become free of it, doing what human beings did for thousands of years: placating the gods to allow human beings certain limited freedoms. This effort does not involve submission and obedience. In "Masks" Picard has to trick the gods in order to be free of them. This is easier to do than it might at first seem, because in *Star Trek* the gods of myth are omnipotent but not omniscient. They can only see the universe through the frame of their particular story, which they repeat over and over again like the story of the sun god Masaka's reluctance to move over and be displaced by the moon. The universe of myth is a kind of prison for the mythological characters who inhabit it, and Picard's mission in "Masks" is to get myths to return to their proper place in a purely mythical world. Though myth was certainly intended to be a point of contact between the human and divine worlds, the aim of most *Star Trek* episodes dealing with myth is not to promote contact. The aim is to close the open door between myth and reality and seal it shut. The only myths allowed in our world are those that are universally acknowledged to be false and powerless, such as the Kahless myth. In "Rightful Heir" the cloned Kahless is defeated in battle by Chancellor Gowron; the fact that Kahless is *not* all-powerful is clearly part of his appeal for Lieutenant Worf, who wants the mythical figure to come right out and admit that he is a fiction. Myth, in the sense of a system of stories posing as a reliable explanation of the world, is only acceptable to the series in its watered-down, alienated form. Worf doubts the divine Kahless, but accepts the discredited Kahless.

The nature of the divine beings seen here also tells a lot about

Star Trek's attitude toward the mythical world. The gods Picard confronts in "Masks" are uniformly cranky and self-absorbed, utterly uninterested in the impact of their decisions upon humanity. They are all-powerful, and they control the basic forces of the universe, the setting of the sun and the rising of the moon, but the fate of humanity is of little interest to them. They are very far from the benevolent creator-god of Christianity or the angry god of Judaism. Though they may assume human form, there is nothing human about them. In "Masks" the crew of the *Enterprise* find themselves squeezed out of their ship by a sudden profusion of stone statuary. The gods of myth uniformly assume the form of monuments, stone, inert, unchanging, and unresponsive to human needs and concerns. It is usually better when these gods ignore humanity and mind their own business. The aim of Picard's plan in "Masks" is precisely this: to return the mythical gods to their own realm and allow humanity to resume its course unimpeded by contact with myth. The implication is that myth, though it can articulate basic truths about the order of the universe, is too dangerous to allow for sustained contact. Most *Star Trek* episodes about myth end with the return of mythical figures to a mythical world. The series sees the mythical world as a kind of prison for mythical figures, a prison from which they occasionally break free. Mythical figures are seen as performing a very important work, a labor such as moving the sun and the moon, but they can perform it only by staying in their own world. The series thus sees an essential separation between the mythical and the actual world. The barrier can be crossed, but it must always be restored. In *Star Trek* myths may have an explanatory value, but only at a distance.

Though *Star Trek* tries to see myths in their own terms, the series avoids sanctioning the reality of the mythical world. In "Masks," as elsewhere in the series, the myths are maintained by a machine.

Myth is usually seen as the last remnant of a civilization, either maintained by some mechanical sentinel or archive (as in "Masks") or studied as artifacts by amateur archaeologists, such as Picard. Myth is something from the past, a strain of story to be studied or a pitfall to be avoided like a shell embedded in an old battlefield. When it comes alive, it generally does so as part of a computer program designed to recreate an old myth, as Kahless is cloned in "Rightful Heir," or a program designed to preserve one, as in "Masks." Very few episodes see myth as actually interpreting a divine world, as serving their traditional function of being a genuine allegory of an adjacent, invisible world. *Star Trek* always views myth's religious function in cultural terms. In the series myth is always seen through the eye of the anthropologist rather than through the eye of the priest. Myth is not a system of absolute truths, but rather a system of variable signs through which a culture interprets its position in the universe. This may seem like a watering down of the original purpose of myths, which were once seen as conduits between human beings and the gods. But *Star Trek* sees myth as performing a vital and underappreciated function: as the central means of communication between races and as the very basis of language itself. Myth may no longer be a language for communicating with the gods, but it remains an essential language. The meaning of myth as language is the subject of what I consider to be the finest episode of the series: "Darmok."

4

In "Darmok" the *Enterprise* goes into orbit around El-Adrel next to a formidable Tamarian ship. A previous starship captain described the Tamarians as a peaceable race, well-meaning but incomprehensible. The Tamarian captain, Dathon, comes on the viewscreen. He smiles in all friendliness and says, "Darmok and Jalad at Tanagra." When Picard asks him what this means, the Tamarian elaborates by saying, "The river Temarc. In *winter.*" Before they can get any farther, Captain Dathon takes out two daggers. As he does, both Dathon and Picard dematerialize in a transporter beam.

The two captains are now alone on the surface of El-Adrel. Dathon tries to hand him a dagger, saying the two names once again. Picard makes no move to accept the weapon, telling him he doesn't want to start a war. Dathon elaborates by saying, "Darmok of Kanza. Jalad of the Kituay." Realizing these are proper names, Picard responds with his own name, but his words mean nothing to the alien.

The next morning the two captains are awakened by a tremendous animal roar. Captain Dathon comes running toward Picard, daggers in both hands. He practically shoves the weapon in Picard's hand, saying once again, "Darmok and Jalad at Tanagra." Some kind of creature is now in the clearing, its presence filling the air with a low electrical crackling. As the creature hovers near them, Dathon cites another name, an army, "with fist closed." Picard finally begins to understand that Dathon communicates by metaphor and example.

The creature attacks again, and the Tamarian is grievously wounded. Dathon is now dying. Again he says, "Darmok and Jalad at Tanagra," but this time his voice has a certain finality, as though the incident with the creature has made its point. From his conversation Picard now puts together the pieces of the myth of Darmok and Jalad at Tanagra. Darmok and Jalad arrive separately at Tanagra, Darmok coming by sea, Jalad by land. They struggle against a beast, and vanquishing it at last, leave together. As Dathon lies dying, Picard tells him a parallel story from earth, a story drawn from the *Gilgamesh* epic of ancient Babylon.

The Tamarian dies just as the *Enterprise* has completed preparations to get its captain back. The *Enterprise* fires on the Tamarian ship, which is now returning fire. The *Enterprise* looks to be hopelessly outgunned. Picard addresses the Tamarian first officer on the viewscreen. When the Tamarian starts to say, "Darmok," he's startled when Picard completes his sentence by saying, "And Jalad. At Tanagra." The aliens are saddened by the news of Dathon's death, but they take out a book in which is written the story of Darmok and Jalad at Tanagra. The first officer picks it up, saying solemnly, "Picard and Dathon at El-Adrel." The Tamarian ship retreats.

It may seem a little flat in the summary, but the acting and filming do justice to the story. The Tamarian captain radiates goodwill. The monster is not too detailed (in science fiction the unknown is always more threatening than the known). And the language of the Tamarians is given a range and richness worthy of the epic. Everything they say is cast in metaphors drawn from a heroic world. "The river Temarc" means the crossing of a boundary. "When the walls fell" means a sudden catastrophic change. "In winter" means a time of sadness. "His arms open" means a willingness to talk. Picard picks up on the epic form when he responds to the Tamarian at the end by telling him the story of Gilgamesh. The death of the alien captain is a very solemn moment, and Patrick Stewart brings his great intelligence to the role of Picard when he tells the dying Dathon, "I understand your sacrifice, Captain."

The idea of a society sacrificing someone to a accord with a story is not so far-fetched as it may at first seem. Almost exactly the same thing happened to the British explorer Captain James Cook when he made first contact with the inhabitants of Hawaii in 1778. On Kauai Cook landed to a royal welcome, and his ship's log, which still survives, is one long testimony to Hawaiian hospitality. After a few weeks, his crew refreshed and his ship provisioned, he went back to sea. Cook always looked forward to returning to Hawaii, and when he did a little over a year later, he and his landing party were slaughtered on the beach where they landed at Kealakekua Bay. What happened in February of 1779 was incomprehensible to Cook and later generations of British explorers, but perfectly comprehensible to the Hawaiians. His rearrival had played exactly into their myth of a returning god. Cook was not killed because of anything he said or did. He was killed to maintain the story, which spoke of not one but two returns of Orono, the god of the harvest. On the first return the god was to be welcomed. On the second he was to be put to death. The Hawaiians were simply acting in accord with their story. This is essentially the same situation as in "Darmok," where the Tamarians view the Federation through the prism of their primary stories. The entire episode is a testimonial to the precedence of story in establishing understanding. Wherever we go, it seems to say, our narratives precede us and explain things for us. They are so important that they must be upheld at any cost. In "Darmok" Captain Dathon sacrifices his life in order to reenact one of his culture's central stories in the company of Captain Picard.

The reenactment need not always be exact, as it was for the Hawaiians in the case of Captain Cook. The simple imperative is that the story be acted out. It does not have to come to the same conclusion every time. In the original version of the Darmok story Darmok and Jalad arrive separately at Tanagra, defeat the beast in battle, and leave together. In "Darmok," however, the story has a different ending. Dathon dies and Picard leaves alone. What is important here is not the exact repetition of the Darmok story but Picard's participation in it. By participating, Picard learns the rudiments of the Tamarian language and culture. When he returns to the bridge of the *Enterprise* in the last minutes of the episode,

Picard is able to speak to the Tamarian first officer in his own language, saying, "The beast at Tanagra." Shaking his head, he adds, "when the walls fell," meaning that Dathon has died. To the Tamarians, Picard's participation in their story is a sign that he and the Federation are ready to join the larger community symbolized by the shared story. For his part, Picard survives the story of Darmok and Jalad at Tanagra to study the Homeric hymns, pondering the shaping influence of our own early myths on the Federation's exploration of outer space.

One remarkable feature of such early mythic stories is that they continue to work on cultures, even after people have stopped believing them to be true. Captain Dathon never makes any claim that the story he is reenacting is true; in *Star Trek* generally myths are neither true nor false. What they are is endlessly reenacted, often using the best technical means available in the twenty-fourth century. In "Darmok" the story of Darmok and Jalad at Tanagra is reenacted using a holographic monster. A similar thing happens in the "Kahless" episodes where a group of Klingon priests clone a messiah; Lieutenant Worf exposes the fraud but decides to endorse it as a means of recovering the old story of Kahless the Unforgettable. In *The Next Generation* the holodeck that has been built right into the hull of the *Enterprise* allows the crew to insert themselves into whatever story they choose. As I said at the beginning of this chapter, the perception behind the need for the holodeck is simple: the farther human beings voyage out into the universe, the more they need to remind themselves of the stories telling them who they are. On the *Enterprise* stories are more than recreation. They are part of the basic equipment of the ship, allowing the crew to particulate in revitalizing exercises of self-recognition through storytelling. But at no point in this exercise of self-recognition does the crew believe the stories told on the holodeck to be true. Story may be essential to cultural identity as the series conceives of it, but it is also essential that stories stay in their place. Fictions seeping into reality are uniformly represented as dangerous in *Star Trek,* and as discussed earlier, dozens of episodes of the series are devoted to returning fictions to the holodeck and restoring the border between fiction and reality. The crew of the *Enterprise* needs the holodeck, but the holodeck needs to be kept in its place.

The theme of "Darmok," then, is the priority of story in explaining the world. The episode ends with Picard in his Ready Room, engrossed in a book. Riker enters with damage reports and asks him what he is reading. "The Homeric hymns," he tells him. "One of the root metaphors of our own culture." Picard goes on to say that "More familiarity with our own mythology might help us relate to theirs." This is perhaps the final message of this episode—that despite the sacrifice of the Tamarian captain to make himself understood, our understanding of our own mythology must inevitably come first because, whether we like it or not, we are immersed in the system of myths we use to explain the world. Little wonder why so much science fiction is mythical in content. Science fiction takes as its great theme the exploration of the universe, leading to first contact between previously unknown races. But in "Darmok" the moment of first contact is not a moment of transparency and clarity but a moment of self-absorption and misinterpretation. The reason is simple: *First contact is through story and myth.* Myths, our fundamental stories devised long ago to explain the unknown, resurface at moments when we are once again faced with the unknown. These are moments like Cook's landing in Hawaii, or, to take an even more familiar example, Columbus's first landing in the Caribbean, where, according to his journals, he decided that the Indians he met on the beach were characters from the biblical narrative of the Garden of Eden. The "Darmok" episode of *Star*

Trek shows that our old stories stay with us whether we like it or not.

But "Darmok" goes even farther than this in the claims it makes for the priority of story. "Darmok" makes a case for the mythic content of language itself. The crew of the *Enterprise* is not familiar with Tamarian stories and so finds it very difficult to communicate with the Tamarians. This gap in communication is not simply due to a lack of knowledge of Tamarian mythology. Difficulties arise precisely because Tamarian myths are embedded in the Tamarian language. The Tamarian language does not simply use metaphors occasionally the way other languages do. The Tamarians speak a language composed wholly of metaphoric references to their mythic stories. Without a key to their mythology, their language is meaningless, for to them language and story are one and the same. As Counselor Troi explains late in the episode, "It's as if I were to say to you, 'Juliet. On her balcony.' If you didn't know who Juliet was or what she was doing on that balcony, the image alone wouldn't mean anything." The officers on the *Enterprise* have to conclude that to have any kind of contact at all with the Tamarians, it would be necessary "to learn the stories from which the Tamarians are drawing these images." To understand the Tamarians, in other words, they would have to become Tamarians, which of course they never can do. The irony is that, even after Dathon's death, the best the crew of the *Enterprise* can hope for is an incomplete and partial understanding of their new Tamarian friends.

There is one greater irony, however. The final irony of the episode is that, for all their strangeness, all Dathon's stories are ultimately derived from our own. Tamarian mythology is, after all, *our* projection of an alien culture. Certainly this episode of *Star Trek* tries very hard to create a culture very different from our own, but it winds up doing exactly what cultures in the same situation have done for thousands of years: casting the unknown in familiar terms by projecting familiar old stories into new contexts. For when it comes right down to it, "Darmok" is essentially a reenactment of the *Gilgamesh* epic in a slightly shifted context. Dathon is Enkidu, the friend of the king who dies killing the Great Bull of Heaven. Picard is Gilgamesh, who mourns him with the words: "He who was my companion through adventure and hardships is gone forever . . ." The surface theme of the episode is the sacrifice of the Tamarian captain for a chance at communication. The deeper theme is much darker. It hints at the impossibility of communication between cultures, suggesting that stories do not successfully communicate meaning between cultures; rather, stories are more of an internal matter, telling an individual culture what it is and often misleading it as to the nature of cultures outside itself. It also points at a phenomenon familiar to students of mythology. Mythologies rarely coexist. Usually, when two mythologies come into contact with one another, one becomes dominant and the other subordinate, much as happened two thousand years ago when Christianity replaced the classical pantheon of Greek and Roman gods. The same process is visible here as a root story from our culture, the story of Gilgamesh and Enkidu, becomes the template for a root story of another, the story of Darmok and Jalad. So even this parable of communication between cultures is dominated by the mythology of one of them—ours—complete with an epic vocabulary remarkably like that of Homer.

"Darmok" is among the very best episodes of *Star Trek*. Not every episode is so tightly wound or so beautifully structured. "Darmok" appeared in the fifth season of *The Next Generation*. It took two series and six movies to work up to an episode as good as this. "Darmok" crosses many boundaries, into literary history, social history, anthropology, and myth. For clarity of examination I have divided this book into four distinct chapters, but in "Darmok" all the fundamental themes of *Star Trek* come together in a single episode. Here is an episode in which you really do need to understand the attitude of the series toward all its basic issues, toward contact and conflict, toward character and identity, and toward story and myth, to see what is going on. "Darmok" begins by positing a society based on a metaphoric language derived from a literary epic. It then recaps a situation often seen during our age of exploration, a cultural misunderstanding through myth, such as that which led to Captain Cook's death. It goes on to offer an anatomy of the classic moment of all anthropology, the moment of first contact. And finally it reveals the shaping power of myth over language and cultural identity. All this is compacted into one episode of a television show aimed at a vast popular audience. No other television show has ever shown this kind of literary or cultural range. The episode is one of the great achievements of the series, and it is now considered a classic. One reliable index is that its major alien character, Captain Dathon, is now sold as an action figure along with Picard and Riker and the rest of the crew of the *Enterprise.* Dathon appears in only one episode of the series, and yet his character, played with subtle restraint by Paul Winfield, is one of the most widely reproduced of the series.

The episode also brings together the basic ideas about story and myth we have seen throughout *Star Trek.* In "Darmok" story assumes its predictable position as a trap as Picard and Dathon are cornered by a monster drawn from a mythical tale. The deadly element of a repetitive story is also in evidence as the monster kills Dathon. And yet there is a redemptive side to story in the episode. As soon as Picard figures out that the story Dathon is trying to tell him is not simply a story but a *myth,* he realizes that he is in different territory. Myths have all the attendant dangers the series usually associates with story, such as entrapment and circularity, but they also have a completely different dimension. This dimension is not the otherwordly point of origin we customarily associate with myth. The episode is notably devoid of references to the reality of the mythic figures it refers to, and there are no moments like those in the various episodes about Kahless where Worf questions the existence of God. Myth in "Darmok" is not a matter of belief in God but of belief in language.

The lack of a divine presence behind mythology in *Star Trek* does not, however, indicate the lack of an overall belief structure in the series. As we shall see in the next chapter, the series rarely misses an opportunity to discredit organized religions. From the high clerics among the Klingons to the priests and prophets among the Bajorans, ecclesiastical structures are uniformly regarded with a suspicion that almost always turns out to be justified. *Star Trek* thus has a recognizably modern attitude toward mythology. In the series the pantheon of gods is at best a thing of the past, or at worst, a complete fraud. But in "Darmok" the series discovers the essentially modern idea that myth is a form of language. As a grammar, myth is not at all deterministic. Picard and Dathon do not exactly reenact the story of Darmok and Jalad at Tanagra; things turn out differently in the episode than they did in the myth. Rather, the point is that myth helps frame language, giving it structure and meaning, and helps make possible the act of communication itself. In "Darmok" myth is the frame for meaning in language, and though future communication between the Tamarians and the Federation may not always take place at the mythic level, myth has the force of initiation. Part of the implication here—an implication borne out by much recent research—is that the telling of myths may have been among the first acts of human language. The need to tell important stories may well have been an early impetus to the development of language itself. In line with this idea "Darmok" places first things first, and in this episode the first of all first things is myth.

In *Star Trek,* then, a myth is more than a mere story. A myth is a story that is built into a language. The Klingons, like the Tamarians, speak by recourse to a constant pattern of reference to their basic myths. Even the experience of the Federation is encapsulated not in a historical narrative but in the series of story/episodes comprising the series itself. Much has been made of Federation history, and various compilations have been issued organizing that history into a time line. But the fact remains that Federation history is not a line of discrete historical events but a collection of stories told one by one, week by week, year after year. Story is the one inescapable reality of *Star Trek.* The crew can be trapped by them, deceived by them, enlightened by them, and sometimes liberated by them. But it is when stories shade into myth that they begin to reveal some of the most basic of human experiences. Foremost among these is the experience of language in one of its earliest forms, the form of storytelling. We have seen how *Star Trek* explores the status of myths without going so far as believing in the myths themselves. *Star Trek* may not believe in its stories in the ordinary sense of conferring reality on a system of mythological beings, but it does have a well-defined structure of belief. Part of *Star Trek*'s system of belief can be seen in its faith in story as the basis for human language. But the series also has another system of belief that can often seem to transcend language. The series is full of events for which there is little or no adequate description in language. These events, and the belief structure that they presuppose, always involve a certain sense of wonder, and they will be the subject of the next chapter.

Chapter Four

the
SENSE
of
WONDER

The universe of *Star Trek* is in many ways a rational universe. Gene Roddenberry's vision of the United Federation of Planets is a vision of rational social progress. In *Star Trek* humanity has straightened itself out and created a functioning galactic democracy. There is little or no sense of religion left among humans; in four series and eight movies, not a single human crew member of any Federation ship professes any form of religious belief. Formal religious belief is something reserved for aliens and is usually a sign of cultural weakness. None of the powerful societies in the *Star Trek* universe have more than a vestige of religious belief. The great rivals and equals of the Federation, the Romulans and the Cardassians, are also technological societies living in a galaxy of *realpolitik*. The Klingons have a religious system they no longer believe in, and their position in the quadrant is clearly slipping. Religion in *Star Trek* is usually reserved for marginal and easily dominated societies such as the Bajorans, who revert periodically to their religion of the prophets and see Commander Benjamin Sisko in *Deep Space Nine* as some kind of emissary from an otherworldly realm. The Bajorans are the most religious race in *Star Trek*, and, apart from a high standing on one of *Star Trek*'s many alternate universes, they are unlikely to hold much of a position of power in this one. Other societies dominated by religion are uniformly seen as handicapped by their illusions. It would seem on the surface that Gene Roddenberry has created a galaxy in which reason is paramount, and revelation has no place at all.

The series, in fact, rarely misses an opportunity to discredit organized religion. In *Star Trek* every standing bureaucracy of clerics is uniformly seen as venal and self-serving. The Klingon clerics of Boreth fabricate a false messiah in "Rightful Heir." A fraudulent devil shows up to fulfill a prophecy in "Devil's Due." The high priestess of the Bajorans seeks to upset the peace of the quadrant in "In the Hands of the Prophets." Even in the case of Spock, organized religion is suspect. In various episodes and movies he submits to various Vulcan spiritual disciplines that involve subjecting himself to bodily deprivation and spiritual isolation. Usually, when he comes out of it, he admits that he has gone too far and wants to rejoin Starfleet as an emissary or ambassador in some important political matter. There is little sense that his periods of contemplative religious activity have actually prepared him to lead a public life. Here, as elsewhere in *Star Trek*, religion is something that must be renounced so that progress in the galaxy can move forward. It would seem that the sense of religion, meaning the sense of a universe suffused with divine agency, would seem to have completely atrophied in the *Star Trek* universe.

So it would seem that *Star Trek* begins with a world in which God is missing. There are many references to religion scattered throughout the series, but most of them form a clear consensus. A belief in the supreme being, or in his evil nemesis, are curiosities from the past. They are part of history and archaeology, but not part of a living faith. Captain Picard says it very clearly in "Who Watches the Watchers?": "We haven't had that kind of belief in hundreds of years." But the series does not stop there, by simply relegating religions to the distant past. In *Star Trek* most religions are frauds. Any number of episodes are devoted to discrediting active religions, rather than anatomizing dead ones. Respect for religious belief is mostly respect for religious stories, not religious faith. These stories are viewed with the usual ambivalence of the series toward the realm of story. On the one hand stories are seen as essential artifacts of a culture, but on the other they are seen as deceptive fabrications. Religion in *Star Trek* would seem to be just another story, belonging by definition to the deceptive realm of story.

But look again. *Star Trek* is, in fact, full of revelation, though of a completely different order than that we usually associate with established religions and their systems of clerics and rituals. *Star Trek* may not go in for clerics and rituals—in fact, the series deeply distrusts them—but in many ways it preserves the essence of the religious experience. The series is taken up with what can be called *the sense of wonder*. The series leans heavily on visions and miraculous violations of natural law. Many of the shows are full of inexplicable events. There are anomalies and disturbances and fluctuations and singularities. In many shows the crew have no idea who or what they are dealing with. The *Enterprise* finds its way into the unknown and must find its way out again. A lot of people have faulted the science of *Star Trek* for being shoddy; Arthur C. Clarke has said that warp drive is impossible. The speed of light may well never be broken, but probability is not what *Star Trek* is about. *Star Trek* is a marvelous journey, and its appeal derives from the traditional devices of the vision, the dream, the legend, and the wonder. Much of the science of *Star Trek* preserves this quality of miracle: the transport of bodies through space and time, the making of food out of thin air, the rapid healing of injury and disease. Warp drive may violate our understanding of natural law, but the series routinely violates even its own understanding of natural law. Warp ten cannot supposedly be exceeded, and yet dozens of episodes show the *Enterprise* exceeding its own specified limits.

This chapter deals with the visionary aspect of *Star Trek*. Sometimes the series deals with familiar themes such as those seen in the previous chapters: exploration and empire, the loss of identity, the status of story. Just as frequently, though, the series is a voyage into the marvelous. "Too many shots of actors gaping at special effects," says *Entertainment Weekly* of one *Star Trek* movie. The magazine is missing the point. Gaping at marvels is what *Star Trek* is all about. Its mission is "to seek out strange new worlds, to boldly go where no man has gone before." This chapter will explain why so much of *Star Trek* is occupied with out-and-out impossibilities, why so many scenes in so many shows are full of crew members gaping at wonders. In bookstores science fiction is often classified under "Science Fiction and Fantasy." Science fiction is the great modern genre of the sense of wonder, and *Star Trek*, though evidently hostile to organized religion, is radically open to the dynamics of religious experience. We have already seen that the series is suspicious of story but open to certain aspects of myth. The sense of wonder is the kernel of the experience of myth, and as we shall see, it is the reason that the series ultimately favors revelation over reason itself.

The episodes featuring the sense of wonder are often some of the worst episodes of *Star Trek*. Sometimes the *Enterprise* gets into such a fix that nothing sort of a miracle can get the ship out of it. In these cases the scripts of the series supply wonders, which usually fall into three distinct categories. These are technologies, monsters, and gods. The series is often criticized for relying too heavily on special effects and strange technologies, on fabulous beings and monsters, on miracles and various godlike beings. I agree that these wonders may push the boundaries of probability, but they are there for a reason. A monster covered in oil rises out of the sludge in "Skin of Evil" and kills Tasha Yar. Picard dies in "Tapestry" and finds that Q is his guide to the afterlife. Humanity is threatened with nonexistence in "All Good Things" and Q transports Picard back to the beginning of time to observe the birth of life on earth. In *Star Trek* the sense of wonder is always a sense of awe at the beginnings and ends of things. Throughout the series the sense of wonder is reserved for experiences that science and technology cannot comprehend, and foremost among these experiences are the experiences of birth and death. Birth and death are life's central mysteries, times when humanity's ability to manipulate the natural world stops short. These births or deaths can be individual or collective, everything from the birth of a child and the death of crew member to the birth of a planet and the death of a species. In *Star Trek* science fiction shades into fantasy at the precise point where life meets death and existence confronts nonexistence. The border between life and death is the border between science fiction and fantasy. There are some enduring mysteries that science, even the advanced science of the future, cannot comprehend. In these cases science is straw, and the only recourse is awe, or a sense of wonder that such things should be.

1

The science of *Star Trek* is mostly fiction. Very few of the realities of current space travel enter into the series. Getting from place to place in space is today a laborious process. *Star Trek* dispenses with the entire process of launching, orbiting, and retrieving spacecraft. There are few spacewalking scenes in the series, certainly nothing to rival the amazing scene in Kubrick's *2001: A Space Odyssey* in which an astronaut is cut loose and drifts helplessly into space. Space in *Star Trek* is the backdrop for human activity. The ordinary setting of an episode in the series is the starship *Enterprise* or one of many planets, and most of the technologies exist for the purpose of getting the *Enterprise* from one setting to another as rapidly as possible. Space travel in *Star Trek* is never a problem, and the many technologies of the series have, by the twenty-fourth century, neatly solved each of the major impediments to space exploration. Replicators do away with the problem of food storage. Transporters do away with the problem of the gravitational pull of planets. And warp drives do away with the problem of the speed of light. So complete is the technology of space travel in *Star Trek* that all technological innovations regarding it are in the past. Refinements are ongoing; Scotty and Geordi La Forge are always trying to squeeze slightly better performance out of the warp engines. But at no point in four series and eight movies is any significantly new form of technology affecting space travel introduced.

The array of technologies in the series is impressive, but it exists for other than technological reasons. Many of the technologies in *Star Trek* were actually developed by the creator of the series, Gene

Roddenberry, for primarily dramatic reasons. In his book on the making of the series Roddenberry says that he devised the transporter to make it easier for his scripts to move from scene to scene. He had noticed that many science fiction shows were slowed down by clumsy docking scenes, by the need to provide a likely form of transport from one scene to the next. The transporter is an immensely efficient scene-changer, allowing characters to move from one set to another without providing for intervening locales. Roddenberry had a similar dramatic rationale for devising warp drive. To make contact with many "strange new worlds," the ship would need to be able to move uncannily fast. The warp engines served the simple purpose of allowing the ship to visit a different section of the galaxy in each episode. In much the same way the ships's replicators functioned as an endless source of props for each episode. No matter where the *Enterprise* was in space, it could create any necessary implements out of thin air. Technologies like the transporter, warp drive and replicators are thus means to a dramatic end. They are part of the stage directions of the series, and by allowing rapid movements through time and space, they help give each episode a certain dramatic unity.

But there is more than a dramatic reason for all the central technologies of the series. They are all are impossibilities, or near impossibilities. The staple technologies in the series have far more about them of magic than of science. The *Technical Manual* issued for *The Next Generation*'s *Enterprise* is a case in point. The manual is full of line drawings of many of the props seen in the series, but none of these drawings have any interiors. There are no isometric drawings giving an exploded view of any of the technologies because there is no real sense of how any of the basic technologies in the series might actually work. The chapter on warp propulsion goes into detail about the various warp speeds from warp factor one all the way to warp factor ten, but when it comes to the attainment of warp drive itself, it says little more than that the warp drive is able to "distort the space-time continuum enough to drive a starship." Few scientists, even those who advocate space travel, now believe that warp drive, or anything like it, is or will ever be possible. The same holds true for all the other central technologies of the series. It might be possible to dematerialize a human body (such as happens at ground zero in a nuclear explosion), but it would not be possible to reconstitute it in a transporter or other device. The dematerialization chambers seen in the classic "A Taste of Armageddon" from the original series, where casualties vaporize themselves voluntarily, are probably closer to the truth of transporting, and the series comes close to recognizing this in *Star Trek: Voyager* when it has the Kaysan use the transporter as a device to carry out capital punishment. Of all the technologies seen in the series only the phasers do not strain credulity, but even these, according to the *Technical Manual,* are based rather mystically on a kind of crystal called "fushigi-no-umi."

Taken in its own terms, then, technology in *Star Trek* is plausible but never realistic. Rather, technology is the most fundamental form of the sense of wonder in the series. Everything about technology in the series is imbued with wonder. There is no such thing as an ordinary action in a show where the crew of a ship can make any known object materialize out of thin air. The series has a kind of ambient sense of wonder about it, a feeling during each episode that we are in a wonderful world. In the original series this ambient sense of wonder is often conveyed by the high thin whistling to be heard whenever Kirk takes an away team to the surface of a planet. In *The Next Generation* the even hum of the ship's engine is part of the background noise of every episode, reminding us at every moment that we are seeing events on a starship. Both series are full of

156

what can be called ordinary wonders, little reminders that we are watching events in a wonderful world. *Star Trek* is careful to insert these little wonders into even the most inauspicious events of everyday life. When Captain Picard goes into his quarters and orders "Tea, Earl Grey, hot" from a replicator, we are subtly reminded that this is no ordinary world. The beds of crew members are always positioned below a glass canopy lit by starlight. Even sinks are concealed by sliding doors. Recreation is always a time for these ordinary wonders, which range from the blue drinks served in the Ten Forward Bar to the intricate phantasms and landscapes summoned by the holodeck. Indeed it is hard to find a scene in all four series and eight movies that does not have some little wonder inserted in it somewhere. Again and again *Star Trek* gives us a world in which the very condition of existence, down to the little details, is instinct with a sense of wonder.

The sense of wonder seen in the series, then, is both small and large. The little wonders may not be matters of life and death, but they condition us to accept a universe in which anything is possible. The ordinary wonders of *Star Trek* all show us that the evidence of our senses can be deceptive. What appears to be thin air can turn into an object by turning on a replicator. And what appears to be an object can turn into thin air by turning off the holodeck. The ordinary wonders of *Star Trek* do more than disclose to us a world of infinite possibility. They suggest a world in which everything is not as it seems. The condition of wonder is metamorphosis, or the changing of state from one state of being to another. All the little wonders of *Star Trek* are essentially little acts of metamorphosis in which objects undergo changes in their shape. This change can take place in any direction, from thin air to solid objects (as in the case of the replicator) or from solid objects to thin air (as in the case of the holodeck). In either case what matters is the changing of shape.

There is some sense in the series, however, that these ordinary transformations have their limits, that changing shape is not tantamount to a complete change of being. Crew members are always complaining that food synthesized in a replicator does not taste as good as the real thing. They also have numerous problems with the holodeck, a technology which, though it can often approximate reality, is prone to breakdown. The little wonders of *Star Trek* can change shape, but they cannot change being.

The great wonders of the series go much farther. The series gives us metamorphoses not only of shape but of being, metamorphoses in which the very essence of a thing is transmuted into something very different. This essential metamorphosis of being is the grounding element of the sense of wonder of the series. When something changes, it changes not just composition but essence. In these cases there is not just a change of shape but a change of being. Changes of shape can be reversed, but changes of being are unidirectional. The little wonders of *Star Trek* tend to be technological in nature, and usually the implication is that what technology can do, it can undo. Almost all the technical problems faced by the *Enterprise* in the series have solutions that can be found in a relatively brief period of time. Life and death can sometimes be reduced to a technical matter in *Star Trek,* and certainly the series is full of scenes in which Dr. McCoy or Dr. Crusher manage to revive a dead crew member. But much more frequently, the barrier between life and death is something that evades exact technical control, and dead crew members are usually not revived through medical intervention alone. Technology clearly has its limits as a wonder in *Star Trek;* even a Federation doctor cannot revive the dead; these powers are reserved for other sorts of beings, beings I will deal with later on.

But technology can sometimes do more than simply change the

shape of things. Sometimes, at the height of its power, it can alter the very essence of things. Life and death are very near to each other in these cases. Most technologies in the series can change the essence of a thing simply by killing it. Ordinary wonders in the series are weapons that can transform life into death, as in the case of phasers and photon torpedoes (which are tellingly shaped like the caskets periodically used for burials in outer space). Extraordinary technologies are technologies that can transform death into life. The first *Star Trek* movie shows V-ger to be one such transformative technology, absorbing a human couple into itself in a wash of life in the final scene. But the best example in *Star Trek* of a wonder-producing device is the genesis device. Developed by Dr. Carol Marcus, the genesis device was capable of creation *ex nihilo*. The device could take uninhabitable planets and provide them with oceans, rivers, lakes, and an atmosphere, all without regard to the distance of any nearby sun. The scenes in *Star Trek II: The Wrath of Khan* showing the creation of a world have an almost biblical majesty. But the device was ultimately a failure, and not simply due to technical difficulties. The evil Khan steals the device, seeing that it can also be used as a weapon. In *Star Trek* it seems that even extraordinary technologies such as the genesis device are always reverting to the status of ordinary technologies such as phasers and photon torpedoes. In the *Star Trek* universe the power to transform life into death is not a power to be held by human beings, but by certain kinds of more powerful beings, gods of sorts, as I will show later on.

But the greatest humanly created technical wonder is not a weapon or some kind of servomechanism but an approximation of human life itself. Unquestionably, technology approaches wonder most clearly in the case of the android. The android is another case of wonder along the borderline between life and death, because, after all, the android is a machine composed of dead matter that has somehow crossed the boundary to achieve a kind of life. The presence of Lieutenant Commander Data in *The Next Generation* is an ongoing testimony to the technological sense of wonder in the series. Data, it seems, is neither exactly living nor exactly dead. Numerous episodes kill him off and then revive him again. In "Thine Own Self" he is dead and buried two meters underground. In "Time's Arrow" his head is severed for four hundred years. Every episode involving Data asks the questions most fundamental to the sense of wonder: What is life, and where does life begin? Crucial to Data, and to the sense of wonder, is that these questions are essentially unanswerable. Data may be alive, but nobody is quite sure exactly how he works. His "emotion chip" turns up in one episode but evades laboratory analysis. And, most important of all, his creation and creator are shrouded in mystery. Though Data supposedly contains an exhaustive record of everything he has experienced, he does not remember his own birth, the moment when he himself crossed from nonexistence to existence. He also speaks of his own death with a certain sense of anticipation, realizing that the experience of birth, aging, and death are the defining and least-understood experiences of humanity. There is a double sense of wonder whenever he appears on the screen, for Data not only seeks answers to the mysterious questions most basic to the sense of wonder, but in a certain sense he is a wonder himself. Data is a wonder-seeking wonder, and it comes as no surprise that his basic effect as a character is a quizzical openness to every new experience, a childlike sense of wonder.

Something too should be said about the technical means by which the sense of wonder is invoked throughout *Star Trek,* namely, special effects. Special effects form a special category of technological wonder in the series. The series is often faulted for too many special effects, or for bad ones. True, the planets made of plaster for the original series look as fake as fake can be. But seen in the right light, they are important elements of the meaning of the series. The fake planets are like creche scenes; they are not supposed to evoke the real world but the presence of an adjacent, invisible one. A planet in the original series usually features strange colors from the spectrum and high-pitched, wailing sounds in the background. The fakiness of the *Star Trek* planets is not the fault of the set designers but the very means through which the series suggests contact with another realm. Nobody could mistake a planet in the original series for a real planet, but here realism is not the point. The settings in the original series have something of the quality of religious kitsch, objects that are also meant to evoke the presence of a nonhuman realm. Stark and unnatural colors also pervade these planets much as they do in kitsch. Here it is worth noting that the original series favored strong and unrealistic contrasts of primary colors, even on the *Enterprise,* which is awash in vibrant reds, blues, oranges, and purples. In contrast, the second *Enterprise,* the NCC-1701D of *The Next Generation,* features a ship of more muted colors: beige and taupe and burgundy and light brown. In keeping with the greater realism of the second ship, there are far fewer godlike beings in the second series. The *Enterprise* of Captain Kirk has a run-in with an omnipotent being in nearly half of its seventy-eight episodes, while the *Enterprise* of Captain Picard confronts omnipotent beings in only a few, mostly those episodes dealing with Q or with the Traveler. There may be gods in the *Star Trek* universe, but they seem to be dying out.

Special effects other than the planet sets also come in for a certain amount of criticism, but special effects are the soul of *Star Trek.* Each special effect is a kind of miracle. Special effects specialize in impossibilities. The quality of miracle is typically enhanced by the way certain scenes are filmed. When Dr. McCoy or Dr. Crusher heals a patient, the camera lingers on an expanse of skin as a beam of light heals a grievous wound. When Lieutenant Worf has a spine transplant, his new spine glows in its enhancement field. Special effects are usually associated with light. In *Star Trek,* as in the Western religious tradition, a beam of light performs miracles. The beam of light may heal a wound, as in the case of an advanced medical instrument. The beam may defeat an enemy, as in the case of a phaser. It may transport bodies from one place to another, as in the case of the transporter. Or it may move a ship through space faster than light itself, as in the case of warp drive. In each of these cases, though, there is a concentrated and focused sense of light emanating from one source and converging on another. Here it should be remembered that most special effects in science fiction are substitutes for physical impossibilities. Any special effect in *Star Trek* is tantamount to an admission that something does not exist or cannot be done. And yet, on the screen, we seem to see an object existing or an action being performed. Special effects always ride the line between existence and nonexistence, thus enhancing the ambient sense of technological wonder basic to the series.

2

But the sense of wonder involves more, much more, than the power of technology. Technology is, after all, nothing more than an array of machines, sophisticated though they may be, and the sense of wonder is always a sense of awe at the presence of life itself in the universe. Lieutenant Commander Data may always strive to attain his goal of becoming fully human, but to become fully human he would have to become a living being, which of course he never can. Technology, especially when amplified by special effects, can approximate the sense of wonder, but it can never fully achieve it. The sense of wonder is a sense of awe at life in whatever form it may take, and in the *Star Trek* universe life takes many forms. The series is full of many other nonhuman life-forms other than the humanoid races, and their lives and deaths are the subjects of many episodes. In particular, the series is full of monsters. Some of these resemble mythical beings, such as griffins, centaurs, and unicorns. But most are exercises of the imagination and have no exact analogue in our history. There are earth-burrowing creatures that pass through rock without effort. There are creatures composed of pure electricity. And there are creatures composed of a single element that has somehow come to life, such as the sludge monster in "Skin of Evil." The monster in *Star Trek* is always allied with the basic mysteries of life and death, and as we shall see, it comes as no surprise that the only death of a major character in the series, the death of Tasha Yar in *The Next Generation,* comes at the hands not of a humanoid or a god but of a monster.

"Monster" is a rather imprecise term to use in describing these beings. Monsters in *Star Trek* may seem in themselves to be wonderful beings, but usually, when the full story comes out, they turn out to have rather mundane origins. The monster in *Star Trek* may show that the universe is full of surprises, but the surprise wears off quickly and the monster becomes yet another species in the pantheon of species in the series. There are no monsters in the series in the sense of an utterly unique being like the Abominable Snowman or the Loch Ness Monster. Monsters in *Star Trek* are generally seen as members of previously unknown species, frightening at first, but less so as they become known over time. The large scaled monster of "Galaxy's Child" turns out to be a mother pregnant with her young. The rock-burrowing creature of "The Devil in the Dark," an episode of the original series, turns out to be female minding a store of eggs. In both these cases the "monster" turns out to be nothing other than a species following its instincts. Still, in both cases the monster appears as a guardian of birth, and birth is always associated with the sense of wonder in the series. The sense of terror experienced on first contact with the monster gives way to a sense of wonder as the monster, at first seen as inimical to life itself, comes to participate in one of life's most basic functions, reproduction. The monster sheds its identity as a horror and becomes yet another form of life in the *Star Trek* universe.

A clear example of this movement from a sense of horror to a sense of wonder comes in "Galaxy's Child." In this episode the *Enterprise* discovers a large spaceborne life-form near the Alpha Omicron system. The creature looks like a large scaled potsticker, and predictably enough, it attacks the *Enterprise.* The ship easily fights off the creature, but in doing so kills it. The creature, however, was pregnant, and Dr. Crusher delivers its offspring by using the ship's phasers to perform a cesarean section on the mother's body. But the resulting infant creature thinks that the *Enterprise* is its mother, and the *Enterprise* must wean the creature and deliver it to an asteroid belt where other members of its species await it. The basic movement in this episode should explain why there is no place for horror in the series. Much other science fiction is full of frightening and completely malignant forms of life; think of the three *Alien* movies. But in *Star Trek* all life is life, and life is never frightening for long. Horror always requires a sense of revulsion, and in *Star Trek* this sense of revulsion is difficult to sustain. Under scientific examination it always turns out that the monsters seen in the series are behaving according to biological predictable patterns. In a very real sense there are no monsters in the *Star Trek* universe, just living beings whose existence has yet to become familiar. Many scenes in the series show a vastly different group of species socializing amiably around a bar, which is an indication of what finally happens to monstrosity in the series. Horror dissipates, familiarity takes hold, and finally a kind of coexistence settles in. Fights do have a tendency to break out in these interspecies bars, but they are certainly more peaceful places than the sites of first contact with the many monsters of the series.

Real monsters in *Star Trek,* then, are few and far between, and when they do appear they often have to do more with death than with birth. Real monsters in *Star Trek* are all totally unique beings, one of a kind, and when they do appear, there is real terror. Totally unique beings are unknown in nature; monsters in *Star Trek* can sometimes appear to be singular, but they uniformly turn out to be survivors of a species or individuals isolated from the pack. A singular being is, in fact, a horror, violating every law of nature, and when one appears in the series, it means trouble. Species monsters in *Star Trek* usually shed their monstrosity by tending to their young and becoming one with all the other species in the universe through the mystery of birth; singular monsters never shed their monstrosity, for they are associated with death. They come to take a human life, and the fear allied with their monstrous appearance is an extension of the fear of death. These unique monsters take a human life, usually the life of a minor crew member, but on one memorable occasion, one of these unique monsters takes the life of a member of the bridge crew, Tasha Yar. These murderous monsters often lack distinct form, or they have a changing form. Their history is a mystery, and unlike the many seeming monsters of the *Star Trek* universe, they cannot be understood, only escaped.

One such monster kills Tasha Yar in "Skin of Evil." Commander Riker assembles an away team composed of Tasha and Crusher and Data to beam down to the surface of Varga Two, where a shuttle carrying Counselor Troi has crashed. There they find the shuttle crashed into a hill, but separating them from the shuttle is an oily black river of scum. Whenever they try to approach the shuttle, the river of scum moves, blocking their path. The black river now congeals into a shroud that addresses the away team. Riker asks permission to pass, telling the shroud that "preserving life, all life, is very important to us." Pressed further, Riker adds, "We believe that everything in the universe has the right to exist." The shrouded creature replies, "An interesting notion which I do not share."

The shroud is *Star Trek*'s version of the Grim Reaper, a representation of death itself in all its horror and wonder. The shroud speaks in a bass voice, telling them that they must not cross the black river. But Tasha has had enough of this. She starts to move toward the river of slime, and as she does, a jolt of energy comes off the river, slamming her down to the ground. Slime covers her face. Beamed up to sickbay and hooked up to every available instrument, she is dead; indicators show no independent brain activity and now all the dials on the panel fall to zero.

The crew of the *Enterprise* must still deal with the monster that killed her, as well as come to terms with her death. The sludge monster tells Counselor Troi that his act of killing Tasha "had no meaning," that he did it "because I wanted to," because "it amused me." There is no attempt here to gloss over the brute fact of her death. Picard and the crew are well aware that she did not die as the result of any extraordinary or heroic action. The series could well have provided Tasha with a warrior's death or given her the opportunity to go down in an act of self-sacrifice. But it did not. Instead "Skin of Evil" gives us the anatomy of a meaningless death. From the moment she dies, Picard and the rest are painfully aware that *she need not have died.* There is no sense of heroic inevitability to her death. "It just killed her," says Dr. Crusher of the monster. "No reason. A senseless, brutal act." But it is the very senselessness of the act that forces them to deal less with the circumstances of her death than with the fact of death itself. In due course the sludge monster is outwitted and finally routed, but the defeat of the monster is not the point of the episode. The point of the episode is to bring the crew up against the absolute barrier between life and death. All the technology and all the know-how of Starfleet cannot prevent Tasha's death or bring her back to life. The crew must look unflinchingly into the face of death.

This they cannot do. The last act of the episode is mostly taken up with mourning the death of Tasha Yar, but there is no funeral, no burial. A holograph of Tasha, which she prepared in the event of her death, appears and addresses the crew, praising each crew member in turn. The scene is a sort of reverse eulogy, with the dead praising the living, rather than the living praising the dead. The emphasis here is not toward the dead but toward the living. There is no sense that Tasha is speaking from beyond the grave. She was there and now she is gone, no one knows to where. The mystery of death persists, but among the living it is mostly felt as a absence.

Many have expressed disappointment with this episode. "The only major *Trek* character ever offed on television," comments *Entertainment Weekly*, "and *this* is how they do it?" It is certainly true that this episode does not have many of the features of an ordinary *Star Trek* episode, which ends with all of the crew revived and well and traveling toward their next adventure in the galaxy. This episode ends with a stark sense of the barrier between life and death. In theory the universe is supposedly an infinite place, but in practice we have seen that in the series it is a much smaller place, hemmed in by empires and uncrossable energy barriers. The infinity of space in *Star Trek* is not quite infinite, and as I said earlier, the series shows very few images of the vastness of space, deciding instead to fill space with ships, stations, and colonies. Death, however, is the one infinity in *Star Trek*. Death is the great barrier in the series, and the sludge monster is a kind of representation of death as the series sees it. The monster melts down into a black river separating life from death. The river sucks Will Riker in, but does not sweep him away; he is restored. But Tasha challenges the river itself and is killed for her hubris. The scene is reminiscent of many Greek myths in which human beings attempt to challenge the inalterable forces of nature and are punished for it. Tasha oversteps the position of human beings in the universe by challenging death itself. But death is not to be avoided, and Tasha dies.

Tasha's death happens about a third of the way through the episode; much of the rest of "Skin of Evil" is devoted to assimilating the fact of her death. The members of the crew are in shock. The only certainty is a kind of stoicism in the face of death. The Stoics were Greek philosophers who believed that death is an unknown and, come what may, must be faced with courage and fortitude. The crew members of the *Enterprise* are similarly stoic in accepting what they know they cannot change. The acceptance, however, is not complete. The working title of the episode was "The Shroud," implying that the sludge monster was a kind of Grim Reaper coming to take Tasha away. The final title of the episode, "Skin of Evil," has a different inflection. Unlike, say, the *Star Wars* movies, *Star Trek* normally eschews extremes of good and evil, choosing instead to posit a more morally ambiguous universe. But here Tasha's death is seen as evil, and the monster that kills her, the incarnation of evil itself. Death is the only true evil in the *Star Trek* universe, where enemies never remain enemies for long; even the Cardassians (in *Deep Space Nine*) wind up being considered for membership in the Federation. The series views death with a combined sense of wonder and horror. The eulogies celebrating her life show the sense of wonder in the face of death, and we never see her body, only a glowing holograph that makes Tasha appear positively angelic. Contemplating Tasha's death gets Data as close to being human as he will ever be, and, in fact, his memory of her is what saves him from being disassembled in "The Measure of a Man." But the monster is horrible and never becomes known and assimilated as a species in its own right; after the episode the planet, Varga Two, is simply declared off-limits to humanity. It is as if it appears in the series solely to kill her, then retires back to the realm of death. The reactions of the crew are muted and stoic, but stoicism in the series can take many different forms. On the death of a fellow Klingon in "Reunion," Worf turns to the sky and screams. Death is horrible, and unlike almost everything else in the *Star Trek* universe, it cannot be explained away. The only true monster in the series is death itself.

Tasha Yar's death, the only death of major character in the series, haunts the next six seasons of *The Next Generation*. In each season there are episodes in which Tasha is remembered or reappears in various ways. Sometimes we see a holographic portrait of her, which Data keeps as one of his prized possessions and takes out from time to time, as in "The Measure of a Man." At other times we see Tasha as her own daughter, a Romulan official named Sela. There is a completely convoluted story about how Tasha's daughter winds up working for the Romulans. Tasha, of course, never had a daughter; she died in 2364 without ever having had a child. Supposedly, though, an alternate version of Yar entered our continuum from some other continuum in 2366, then went into the past, where she gave birth to Sela. The twists and turns of this story do not make for a very clear tale—and believe me, this is about as clear as the story gets—but they do amplify the sense of mystery surrounding the death of Tasha Yar. The normal relations of time and space become unintelligible when faced with the fact of death, and

Star Trek, normally so adept at handling such complex stories, can only respond with a knot of narrative that is not to be unraveled. The mystery, and the sense of wonder at death itself, is increased by the reaction evident on the faces of the bridge crew when they see Sela. Their faces ashen and they grow very still. It is as if they are seeing a vision from beyond the grave, and in a sense they are. Tasha has crossed over to a realm where the rules of time and space no longer apply. The series may be notoriously flexible when it comes to bending those rules, but in the case of death it would seem that no such laws of nature apply. We may never understand how such things can be. In "Eye of the Beholder" Lieutenant Worf puts this sense of the limits of human understanding very well: "There are things we do not understand, yet they exist nonetheless."

This sense of the limits of human understanding is also a sense of the limits of representing the things we do not understand. Episodes probing the central mysteries of birth and death push toward the edge of representation. The ability to tell stories depends on the ability to construct narratives in a linear fashion. In a very real sense there is a breakdown of story when confronted with the fact of death. A death may take place in time, but the reality of death is nonlinear and atemporal, and it frequently disrupts the ability of the series to tell a good story, which is why the episodes dealing with birth and death are not among the best episodes of *Star Trek.* Religious art is notoriously nonlinear and atemporal in its effort to represent a realm beyond space and time, and those episodes of *Star Trek* dealing with the mystery of death also partake of this sense of disruption of our ordinary world. The universe may not be seen as sacred in *Star Trek,* but a death is always seen as sacred because a death is final and the series has a great respect for final things.

Episodes teem with the last survivors of colonies, civilizations, and species. One great constant of the *Star Trek* universe is that all things come to an end, and the galaxy is full of evidence that once-vital cultures flourished and declined. These cultures may try and evade the finality of the end by sending out probes (as in "The Inner Light") or archives (as in "Masks"), but the end is always final and the surviving stories are at best mere fractions of their original wholes. All things must pass, with an exception or two.

3

These exceptions are gods. These are not gods in the accepted sense of a supreme being who originally created the universe. Most of the time *Star Trek* posits a polytheistic universe in which a variety of powerful beings inhabit a realm above and beyond humanity. These gods are omnipotent but not omniscient, and the distinction is important. Gods in *Star Trek* can do anything they want, but they do not always know what to do. A god in a monotheistic universe tends to be seen as solemn, balanced, and decisive. Gods in a polytheistic universe tend to be seen as quarrelsome, capricious, and indecisive. Both kinds of gods appear in *Star Trek,* and mostly, even when working for the good, they tend to be seen as annoyances to humanity. Captain Kirk is peeved when a race of benevolent godlike beings stops an impending war between the Federation and the Klingons in "Errand of Mercy." And Captain Picard finds Q incredibly frustrating on his every appearance. In both cases a god or gods acts as a stay on the human freedom that the series values so highly. The *Star Trek* universe may have an element of divine comedy in it, both ridiculous and sublime, but humanity is not laughing. Gods may exist, but in *Star Trek* it seems that all we want them to do is leave us alone. "Leave us," Captain Picard tells Q at the end of "Encounter at Farpoint." "We have passed your test."

The fully benevolent kind of god is found only rarely in the *Star Trek* universe. Gods in *Star Trek* generally inhabit a realm not sacred but very profane. Gods are distinguished from humanity on the basis of power, not godhood. Q has all the powers of a divine being but absolutely none of a divine being's aura of sacredness. Though there is a suggestion of the sacred in Q's association with the mysteries of life and death, there is actually very little room in *Star Trek*'s rational universe for the sacred. Quests for the sacred tend to degenerate into contests of power, as in the case of Kahless, the Klingon messiah, whose return occasions a power struggle within the Klingon Empire. The sacred sense of all life as instinct with divine meaning and purpose is generally seen as a remnant of a primitive culture, subject to the nonparticipation decree of the Prime Directive. The Federation is itself religionless and Starfleet members participating in the religions of alien cultures are often censured for having perverted the Prime Directive; usually the *Enterprise* is sent to extract them and rectify the situation, as in "Bread and Circuses," where a Federation citizen has defected to a sort of Roman Empire, or "Patterns of Force," where another Federation citizen has modeled a society on Nazi Germany. The one partial exception to this absence of benevolent sacred divinity is the Traveler, who appears in "Journey's End" to guide Wesley Crusher toward a new realm of being. At one point the Traveler asks Wesley what he considers sacred, and Wesley gives a typical Starfleet answer: "I don't really consider anything sacred." In this episode Wesley winds up quitting Starfleet Academy and joining the Traveler on a quest for the sacred, but when he does so, he effectively disappears from the series. Though there are sacral overtones to the sense of wonder, the sacred itself simply has no place in *Star Trek.*

Wesley's spiritual quest is unusual in *Star Trek,* and it is significant that he is a minor character. At the point at which Wesley meets up with the Traveler in "Journey's End," he has been absent from the *Enterprise* for several years. Most of the major characters do not engage in spiritual quests, and when they do, as in the case of Worf, they get very mixed results. Wesley's quest is one of the few represented favorably, and for several reasons. He is a very young man, unformed and immature, and his religious quest is aligned with his need to discover his position in the adult world. But even more importantly, he is guided by a god ideally suited to the mission of the *Enterprise.* The Traveler is a mobile divine being, a god without a home (even a nebulous home, such as the Q Continuum), and *Star Trek* does not favor sedentary gods. On the contrary: its gods are peripatetic beings who wander the universe. Gods worshipped in stationary locales in the series, such as temples or churches, tend to be represented as vestiges of primitive rituals. It is no accident that the divine being most favorably represented by the series is called the Traveler. The Traveler is a god of travel, of journeys and marvelous voyages, a superintending spirit who impels humanity on to new planets and further discoveries. Wesley may leave Starfleet, but it seems that his spiritual mission will be taking him on a parallel course.

The Traveler is also favorably represented because he seems driven by his own sort of Prime Directive. The Traveler refrains from meddling with human affairs. He does not attempt to direct or alter Federation history, as Q does, but impels Wesley to withdraw from it. The series takes a dim view of any sort of divine intervention, and views gods as sort of the ultimate violators of the

Prime Directive, which, taken as a categorical imperative, would forbid powerful beings from interfering with the lives and destinies of less powerful beings. Q is of course the clearest example of this flaunting of the Prime Directive by gods, and I will deal with him shortly. But many other far more benevolent and far less capricious beings are viewed equally severely by the series. In an episode of the original series, "Errand of Mercy," a race of benevolent omnipotent beings called the Organians intervene and stop an impending war between the Federation and the Klingon Empire. As the title of the episode implies, the Organians are a race of merciful gods, gods perfectly suited to their role as arbiters in the universe. And yet they infuriate Captain Kirk, who would rather go to the death than submit to the will of any god. The episode turns out well, with peace prevailing, but the comic ending is the result of a mandated divine comedy. Here divine comedy is infuriating to human beings, who would prefer a free fight to a constrained peace. Even Armageddon is preferable to a loss of freedom.

Extreme as it may seem, this episode actually offers a scenario typical of the series as a whole. Literally dozens of *Star Trek* episodes teem with human resistance to various divine imperatives. Human beings are an impetuous and unrestrainable species, and in the first series William Shatner does a wonderful job of portraying the unsinkable Captain Kirk, whose indomitable human spirit triumphs over every adversity. Kirk's fury is directed particularly at those who threaten human freedom, and though Patrick Stewart portrays a more restrained captain in Jean-Luc Picard, his Picard is every bit as concerned with maintaining and augmenting the human capacity for freedom. Picard may be a very reserved man, but the one character in *The Next Generation* most likely to anger him, and to elicit from him a passionate defense of humanity, is Q. Q is the very archetype of the meddlesome supreme being the series distrusts so deeply. Like the Traveler, he is a peripatetic god who wanders the universe. Unlike the Traveler, though, Q is utterly fixated on the fate of humanity. The Traveler singles out Wesley Crusher as a kind of saint-in-the-making and appears to be willing to let humanity as a whole seek and find its own fate, but Q always appears to put humanity itself on trial. It is no accident that the first and last episodes of *The Next Generation* show Q putting humanity on trial. More than anything else, Q is there to interrogate the ambitions of human beings, and to remind them of the wonders, both savage and sublime, lurking in the universe.

Q shares certain features with the other godlike beings in the *Star Trek* universe. He assumes human form, though he is not human and comments frequently on the limitations of the human body. He is also not very forthcoming about what he knows about the structure of the universe; he regards human intelligence as limited, and the one word he regularly uses to describe human mental capacity is "puny." But if human capacity is puny, human aspiration is not. That is why Q also adopts an attitude of guardianship toward human beings, a guardianship that cuts both ways, both benevolent and judgmental. On the one hand he often appears to warn Picard that human beings have no idea what they are getting into as they expand into the galaxy. On the other he often appears to say that this expansion has its price. Humanity is perfectly capable of disturbing the universe and destroying itself, and Q frequently shows up to say that humanity has gone too far. There is a good reason why *The Next Generation* begins and ends with episodes showing an omnipotent being putting humanity on trial. Humanity may have infinite aspirations, but those aspirations can summon dangers the likes of which human beings can scarcely imagine.

The first of these two trials comes in the very first episode of *The*

Next Generation. "Encounter at Farpoint" makes Q into a very capricious god indeed. He kidnaps the bridge crew and subjects them to a kangaroo court. This court does not charge the crew with any specific crime. Rather Q puts the crew of the *Enterprise* on trial for disturbing the universe. But the trial is a spectacle, a show trial of sorts, and Q is not a very convincing judge. By the second trial at the end of the series, Q has taken on a more serious presence. He has earned the status of a protector of the *Enterprise,* and Picard in turn has protected him, even sheltering him briefly (in "Déjà Q") during his short expulsion from the Continuum. And though the charges are roughly the same, seven seasons of the series have given us ample reason to question humanity's impact of the universe. In seven seasons we have seen human beings repeatedly fracturing the space-time continuum, and employing a technology, warp drive, that pollutes space. We have seen the Federation repeatedly, if not routinely, violate its own Prime Directive. After seven seasons of *The Next Generation,* human beings have really done enough to warrant a trial, and "All Good Things" gives us the great final trial of the series.

The trial, however, does not take place in a courtroom. The trial in "All Good Things" is a trial in the older sense of the word, a test of skill and a moral challenge. In many ways the finale of the series is all previous *Star Trek* episodes rolled into one, and the episode contains all the themes examined in detail in the chapters of this book. In "All Good Things" Picard must deal with the devastating impact of the Federation's exploration of the galaxy, a form of devastation he has unleashed despite the Prime Directive. He must explore his own identity in three different time frames: past, present, and future. He must move rapidly between three different stories, each of which claims to be true and each of which is at least partly false. And he must confront birth and death on a vast scale as he travels to the beginning of life on earth and faces the possibility that humanity may never come into existence. "All Good Things" does more than put humanity on trial. The episode shows a breakdown of all the different barriers underlying the structure of the *Star Trek* universe.

That universe, as we have seen in numerous instances, has a peculiar but consistent structure. The *Star Trek* universe is full of separate but adjacent realms. In the *Star Trek* all manner of time frames, spatial dimensions, and fabulous beings exist, but they must be kept apart from one another. Existence does not mean coexistence. Indeed in episode after episode it is precisely the collision of these different realms that must be averted, and "All Good Things" tests the barriers separating the different times, dimensions, and life-forms of the universe. In this final episode, as elsewhere in the series, *Star Trek* views the universe as full of barriers that one crosses at one's peril. These barriers may be historical, spatial, or spiritual. Historical barriers involve time travel and threaten disruption of the space-time continuum. Spatial barriers involve alternate universes and threaten implosion of different dimensions. And spiritual barriers involve divine beings and threaten breakdown of the hierarchy of species. In each of these cases a different realm of time, space, or being exerts pressure on our universe, and the *Enterprise* finds itself at the pressure point. In each the mission of the *Enterprise* is to read the danger signs correctly and restore the barriers between us and whatever different time, space, or being is involved. As I have said before, the *Star Trek* universe, though supposedly as infinite as space itself, actually views infinity as a dangerous thing. Humanity must learn to live in its allotted sector of space, and, large as that may be, any overleaping of the human realm immediately spells trouble.

Perhaps the worst cataclysm the *Star Trek* universe has to offer is this collision of adjacent universes. According to the science of the series, if two drastically different kinds of matter occupy the same space, both are destroyed. Similarly, if adjacent universes collide, there is mutually assured destruction. This is the real reason why the *Star Trek* universe is so full of demilitarized zones and uncrossable energy barriers. More than anything else, the mission of the *Enterprise* is to patrol these barriers and maintain the integrity of the universe. Those who cross the borders of these basic barriers of being are seen as great threats who must be returned to their own realm. Any being who can cross these barriers at will necessarily poses a danger to the galaxy, no matter how well intentioned that being may be. They must be repatriated to their own realm at all costs, as in an episode of the original series, "The Alternative Factor," where an alien named Lazarus escapes from an alternative universe and must be returned via a dimensional corridor. Every episode of *Star Trek* thus ends with the return of beings to their own space or time and with a restoration of the basic borders of the universe. There is a sense of wonder at the existence of all these realms, but also a sense of relief at returning these realms to their own proper place in the universe.

All these different realms collide in "All Good Things." The episode is like a catalogue of *Star Trek*'s favorite cataclysms. The episode is a superb exploration of the dangers of adjacency. Right from the beginning the basic barriers of the universe seem to be eroding. Captain Picard starts time-shifting between three different frames of reference in the past, present, and future. The past is seven years back, when he first took command of the *Enterprise*. The future is twenty-five years hence, when his crew has moved on to other assignments or left Starfleet. Shifting every few minutes between time periods, Picard has to put together an explanation for what is happening to him. Picard has no idea what is going on until

Q appears and tells him that he has been moving him around through time. Picard is understandably angry, but Q claims that he is shifting Picard around for his own good, and for the good of humanity. Q goes on to tell Picard that Picard alone is responsible for the wholesale destruction of humanity.

Picard must now find out how, and why. The cataclysm destroying humanity has been inadvertently unleashed by Picard in a very strange way. In the future it seems that the *Enterprise* encounters a spatial anomaly and, seeing the fissure as a danger to the stability to space and time, tries to close it by using an inverse tachyon pulse. But the tachyon pulse has the effect of enlarging the fissure in a very unexpected way. The anomaly grows larger, but in the opposite direction of ordinary time, and in time it will engulf earth while the planet is still in its infancy, effectively preventing the evolution of mankind. Still shifting rapidly between time frames, Picard manages to put together the story and coordinate the actions of three *Enterprise*s in three different time frames. Past, present, and future come together as the three *Enterprise*s act in unison and seal the rift the space. As usual, points of contact between different realms of the universe are flash points that lead to crises, crises that can only be resolved by the restoration of the barriers basic to the universe. At the end of the episode Q appears to claim credit for helping humanity, this not as judge but as guardian and mentor.

Q's final appearance in "All Good Things" makes much the same point he has been making throughout *The Next Generation*. He stresses the insufficiency of conventional rational explanations of the universe. "You have no idea how far you still have to go," he tells Picard at one point. He goes on the invoke the two elements of the sense of wonder we have always seen in *Star Trek:* the presence of wonder and the possibility of terror. The very essence of a wonder is that it is a thing so powerful that it can also be horrible. Q rightly perceives that human beings are a curious species searching the universe for new wonders. But his every appearance in *The Next Generation* serves one overriding purpose: to warn the crew of the *Enterprise* that the reverse of wonder is horror, that every wonder is a potential horror. This is the essence of his warning delivered in the last moments of "Encounter at Farpoint." This is also the reason he transports the *Enterprise* into Borg space in "Q Who?", to show that not all newly discovered species are instinct with wonder alone but can also contain a considerable element of horror. And this is the rationale for his final intervention, seen above in "All Good Things." The title of the final episode is itself part of Q's warning: *All good things must come to an end.* It means not only that the Federation is a finite undertaking that must ultimately come to an end, but it also means that the presence of all good things, seen in most concentrated form in the sense of wonder, must too come to an end and be supplanted by its opposite, the sense of horror. These horrors may be small or large, small as a single monster or large as a whole species, but the ultimate horror is, of course, the end of humanity itself.

The senses of wonder and horror are neatly conjoined in a remarkable scene in "All Good Things." Q has taken Picard back through time to primordial earth. Q directs Picard's attention at a small muddy pond. "Right here," he tells Picard, "life is about to form on this planet for the very first time. A group of amino acids is about to combine and form the first protein." Here the wonder of life being formed for the very first time on earth is supplanted by Picard's sense of horror that he, and he alone, disrupted the beginning of life on earth by causing the spatial anomaly to expand into the past.

As always in *Star Trek,* individual human action matters, and matters deeply. *"You* destroy humanity," Q tells Picard at one point. The actions of one man can be responsible for the death of a species. And as always in *Star Trek,* the series eschews the determinism of large historical forces. Picard and Kirk are always saving the universe, and they save it so often that they actually joke about it when they meet in *Star Trek: Generations,* when Kirk says, "I was out saving the universe before you were born." The joke is funny, but the premise underlying it is truly remarkable: one man can save the universe, and conversely, one man can destroy it. Vast as the *Star Trek* universe is, the series posits a universe in which human beings never come to be dwarfed by their discoveries. The universe may be full of thousands of species and millions of planets, but at any point in the series the fate of the universe can hinge on the actions of a single solitary individual. Humanity, individually and collectively, matters, and though there may be many more powerful divine beings in the universe, their very divinity constrains them from acting with the full freedom that human beings possess. Even Q is clearly hemmed in by a series of constraints placed on his powers by the Continuum. Human beings may not be gods, but they are freer than gods, and it is precisely their freedom that gives them great power. Gods in the series are often prisoners of their own divinity, and they are often shown to be voyeurs who enjoy observing humanity, in fact, almost seeming to require human activity to stave off the boredom of immortality. This can be seen throughout the series, from an episode of the original series, "The Gamesters of Triskelion," where three godlike brains amuse themselves by placing bets on fights staged between humans, to a recent episode of *Star Trek: Voyager* in which Captain Janeway is taken to the Q Continuum, which is shown to be a shack full of senile old people living in a desert. Powerful beings in *Star Trek,* despite their peevishness and seeming capriciousness, are actually fairly predictable, and they tend to enjoy observing human beings because humanity, being genuinely free, is genuinely unpredictable. Gods may be all-powerful, but humanity is all-free.

Despite Q's guiding presence in "All Good Things," then, humanity is radically free. Humanity cannot be destroyed by any god. Humanity can only bring destruction upon itself. "I am not the one who causes the annihilation of mankind," Q tells Picard. "You are." Q may be much more powerful than any human being, but his many appearances throughout *The Next Generation* do not strip human beings of their freedom. Rather, Q comes to the *Enterprise* to remind them that their freedom has no limits and, as such, can be limitlessly abused if they are not careful. At no point does Q direct Picard's action or force him to do anything he does not want to do. Q is there to show humanity that it can destroy itself, and, in fact, the *Star Trek* universe is full of extinct species and dead planets that have done exactly that. The *Star Trek* universe is full of ruins, but one species rarely annihilates another in *Star Trek*. These species and worlds freely destroyed themselves, and the repeated presence of their ruins acts as a warning to humanity not to abuse its freedom.

The freedom of humanity to dispose of the universe as it wishes is the real reason for Q's many appearances throughout *The Next Generation*. "The trial never ends," he tells Picard at the end of "All Good Things," for there is no end to human freedom and thus no end to human responsibility. Q is there to remind the crew of the *Enterprise* that all human actions, however thoughtless, have consequences. Even in episodes where the fate of the universe does not hang in the balance, the theme remains the same. In "Tapestry" Q forces Picard to come face-to-face with the consequences of certain thoughtless actions of his youth. Not only is human action far-reaching: *Every human action, no matter how small, matters.* There may or may not be life after death according to the series, but the series definitely preserves the quality of judgment in which every human action is remembered and finally weighed out according to a great divine scale of justice. The seven seasons of *The Next Generation* end with this last judgment, delivered by Q with a curious mixture of open-endedness and finality:

> We wanted to see if you had the ability to expand your mind and your horizons, and for one brief moment, you did . . . For that one fraction of a second, you were open to options you'd never considered. That's the exploration that awaits you, not mapping stars and studying nebulae, but charting the unknown possibilities of existence.

As a judge, it turns out that Q is oddly fair, unexpectedly impartial. Though in both "Encounter at Farpoint" and "All Good Things" he initially appears to have prejudged humanity, Q turns out to be a decent jurist who acquits humanity of his trumped-up charges. But those charges are not exactly as exaggerated as they may appear to be, for Q has ample opportunity to prove that humanity has the power to destroy itself and possibly the universe as well. Nor does he actually acquit humanity of all crimes. Q, rather, gives humanity something like a stay of execution. There is no sense of predestination in Q's sitting in judgment upon mankind. The fate of humanity remains an open question. This is the real logic behind Q's name: Q is, after all, short for Question. In the person of Q humanity faces far more questions than answers. Episodes involving Q pose certain questions with great insistence: Who are human beings? What is humanity's impact on the universe? How far does our knowledge go?

The presence of Q and his troubling and unanswerable questions affirms the presence of mystery and its allied sense of wonder, even in the twenty-fourth century, a century filled with scientific answers to nearly every question imaginable. The presence of Q is a testimony to the limits of scientific rationality in a society defined by it. *Star Trek* may at times seem to favor reason over revelation, but when it comes right down to it, the series does not trust reason too far. In the *Star Trek* universe reason always requires revelation as a stay against a lifeless rationality. Wesley Crusher experiences Starfleet as technologically sophisticated but spiritually dead and finds that he needs to leave Starfleet Academy and join the Traveler. The most logical and reasonable characters in the series are unquestionably Spock and Data, and yet these are precisely the ones most likely to pose disturbing philosophical questions about the nature of the universe. The *Star Trek* universe actually needs a being like Q, an all-powerful being not reducible to any genus or species, to ask the questions that Starfleet cannot ask, let alone answer. We have already seen that Starfleet, at its highest levels, is a very questionable institution full of backbiting and intrigue. Godlike beings such as Q and the Traveler exist to remind the crew of the *Enterprise* that the known universe, large as that may be, is dwarfed by what remains to be known. Q opens new and often dangerous horizons, as when he introduces humanity to the Borg. Gods in *Star Trek* are there to beckon humanity toward the unknown, and to cry a warning of the mysteries to come.

These many mysteries of the universe can often seem overwhelming, and at times the only possible response to them is the open-mouthed awe seen in so many episodes. But there is another response. The mysteries of life and death abide, but so does courage and striving in the face of them. The Federation of *Star Trek* cannot rest from travel through the galaxy. Humanity is always roaming, and in four series and eight movies human beings have seen strange planets and strange manners, thousands of forms of life, government, and culture. And yet there is a basic lack of satisfaction at the heart of humanity, a dissatisfaction at what is known that gnaws at us, pushing us into the untraveled realms of the galaxy. There is no end to human activity in *Star Trek* as starship after starship makes its way toward the margins of the known universe. The barrier of death may never be crossed, but every other barrier in the galaxy beckons to be sought and overcome. Humanity in *Star Trek* has left its home, the earth, a home to which it does not frequently return. One generation of explorers may grow old exploring the galaxy and die, but it is supplanted by a "next generation" of explorers taking up the banner anew. The continuity of generations is very important to *Star Trek*. In four series and eight movies we see Captain James T. Kirk and his crew aging and dying, but we also see a new generation rising to take their places in a new *Enterprise*. The mystery of death may remain, but the wonder of life, ever-renewed life, abides, as humanity, always striving, never yielding, makes its way into the universe.

AFTERWORD

Star Trek is not over yet. The voyages of the starship *Enterprise* may have ended with the last episode of *The Next Generation,* but new generations of Starfleet officers are carrying the mission of the Federation out into the galaxy. Gene Roddenberry died in 1991, and though his creation had by then taken on a life of its own, the *Star Trek* universe has since moved in a new direction. The first series and the first six movies, which culminated in the peace treaty between the Federation and the Klingons in *Star Trek VI: The Undiscovered Country,* essentially perfected the dynamics of an intergalactic balance of power. *The Next Generation* takes place during the heyday of that balance of power, leading to a sense of an intricate standoff between the major powers, a standoff finessed by the Federation's master diplomat, Jean-Luc Picard. But *Star Trek: Deep Space Nine* and *Star Trek: Voyager* usher in a world in which the Federation's confidence in its own mission is undermined by a changed political situation. *Deep Space Nine* faces the challenge of a settled location and many new peoples. *Voyager* confronts a galaxy in which, for all intents and purposes, the Federation does not exist because the ship is lost in space and is no longer in contact with its home ports. In a great many ways space in *Deep Space Nine* and *Voyager* is a far more uncertain and insecure place than it was in *The Next Generation.*

By the seventh season of *The Next Generation,* there are clear signs that the *Star Trek* universe is changing, and not for the better. The second-to-last episode of *The Next Generation* shows the Federation in a very different light than seen previously. In "Preemptive Strike" Starfleet is poised to wage a preemptive strike against the Maquis, a guerrilla organization whose activities on the Cardassian border threaten to upset the balance of power in the quadrant. The plan is to use the recently promoted Lieutenant Ro Laren as a spy. Her mission is to infiltrate the Maquis organization, using her past disciplinary troubles with Starfleet to lend her a certain credibility. She agrees to take on the mission, less because of her political loyalties, which remain with the Maquis as they struggle to throw off the Cardassian yoke, than with Captain Picard, who in the past has acted as her mentor through many difficult days.

For a time the plan goes smoothly. Ro gains entrance to a Maquis cell and quickly wins the trust of its leader, Macias. Soon Ro herself starts to suffer from a classic case of divided loyalties. On the one hand she is aware that she is a Starfleet officer, sworn to uphold the laws and values of the Federation. On the other she is a Bajoran with an instinctive sympathy for the Maquis and their cause. The episode culminates in Ro having to choose between the two. Ro convinces the Maquis to attack a convoy passing through Federation space, while Picard and his ships take up a position nearby, hidden in the Hugora Nebula. But just as the Maquis are about to fall into the trap, crossing out of the demilitarized zone and into Federation space, Ro has a change of heart. She signals the Maquis fleet by firing a low-intensity particle beam into the nebula, thus exposing the hidden Federation fleet. The Maquis fleet turns and escapes, and Ro escapes with them, now a genuine Maquis herself.

The interest of "Preemptive Strike" is that the Federation no longer occupies a position of political or moral authority. Politically, the Federation has traded away many worlds simply to ensure its own stability. Here the calculations forced by the balance of power are calculating and almost mercenary; Starfleet, it seems, will do almost anything to ensure political parity in the quadrant, including consigning many of its citizens to effective slavery. Morally, too, the Federation is wanting. This is the only episode of *The Next Generation* in which Captain Picard appears in a morally questionable light. In one remarkable scene Ro meets with him in a bar to beg to postpone the operation. Picard quickly senses her divided loyalty and threatens to have her court-martialed if she sabotages the operation in any way. He even arranges to have Commander Riker pose as a relative to accompany her back to the Maquis and make sure she carries out her orders. In the bar Ro poses a prostitute as a cover for her conversation with the captain. As Picard pressures her to follow her Federation orders, he punctuates his conversation with loud negotiations for the price of her body. The implication of the parallel is clear. Ro will not prostitute herself; she is not for sale. Picard is acting as a kind of procurer for prostituted loyalty, and in the end he is proved to be acting in the wrong as Ro foils the Federation trap and escapes with the Maquis force. For the first time in the history of *Star Trek,* it seems that the Federation may be on the wrong side of a conflict.

Deep Space Nine shows the *Star Trek* universe in an equally stark and unflattering light. This is the first *Star Trek* series to take place in a fixed location, a space station outpost near Cardassian space. Despite the title of the series, the space station's location is not actually in deep space. *Deep Space Nine* is actually located in a settled area of the galaxy, a place much like the Middle East, a place full of old peoples nursing ancient enmities. There the Cardassians and the Bajorans have a long-standing history of conflict, and the space station is frequently a place of intrigue and subterfuge. The station has some of the sleazy qualities of a border town, and its central feature is not a bridge, which emphasizes command and control, but a promenade and a bar (Quark's Bar), where different races mingle and crowds gather. Maintaining control over the station is not an easy task, and a large part of Commander Benjamin Sisko's job is surveillance. Often he finds that he must rely on a large network of informers maintained by Constable Odo. Ordinary Federation procedures do not always seem to apply to *Deep Space Nine,* and significantly, the station was not built by the Federation but by the Cardassians, who used it as a mining station orbiting the planet Bajor. There is thus always a slightly alien quality to the station. The instruments all over the station are lettered in Cardassian, and the station's interior is full of dark and irregular surfaces, very much unlike the evenly illuminated, smooth interior of a starship. In *Deep Space Nine* humans seem no longer to be in their own world and find that they must adapt to a built environment constructed by an alien race.

That environment seems to be becoming more and more alien all the time. In some ways *Deep Space Nine* shows the breakdown of the *Star Trek* balance of power. The Klingons are on the move again and may not remain Federation allies for long, and the position of Lieutenant Worf is especially insecure. The Dominion and their allies, the Jem'Hadar, may be infiltrating earth. It is no accident that an episode of *Deep Space Nine,* "Gabriel," shows Commander Sisko visiting a troubled period during earth's twenty-first century. The series almost never shows how our world manages to develop into the utopian world of the Federation, but an episode like "Gabriel," which shows Sisko dealing with urban unrest in San Francisco, reveals that the world of *Deep Space Nine* has a certain affinity with times of uncertainty and social change. Unquestionably, *Deep Space Nine* is the most urban of the *Star Trek* series, and the space station itself is often an unruly place requiring the police services of

Constable Odo. *Deep Space Nine* shows that the balance of power, a balance, as we have seen, so characteristic of *Star Trek,* to be constantly on the verge of breaking down. The station is always on the brink of war and conflict, and the sense of wonder frequently gives way to a sense of foreboding. A revival of religious feeling is frequently to blame as waves of religious nationalism sweep both the Klingon and Bajoran home worlds. More rationalistic societies, such as the Cardassians and the Federation itself, now seem to occupy a more insecure position in the quadrant, and the prospect of an indefinite peace, the great goal of *The Next Generation,* seems to be eroding.

The status of rationalism in the *Star Trek* universe can be seen especially clearly in one role played by Commander Sisko aboard *Deep Space Nine,* the role of emissary to the Bajorans. The role of emissary has been conferred upon him by the Bajoran religious clerics. Typically for *Star Trek,* a variety of episodes, such as "In the Hands of the Prophets," show the Bajoran priests to be hungry for power, but Sisko is also aware that the title they have conferred on him has an intangible quality not easily reduced to power politics. Sisko does not want the title, but he finds that in the greater interests of peace in the quadrant, he must tolerate the role and perform it to the best of his abilities. Here a Starfleet officer must act as a cleric in an alien religion, a clear violation of the Prime Directive, the great rational rule of the Federation that mandates noninterference in the development of alien cultures. Starfleet, however, does not forbid Sisko's participation in Bajoran religious rites, but actively encourages it. The startling implication is that Starfleet's interpretation of the Prime Directive may be changing. No longer are its officers forbidden from meddling in alien cultures. Recall that the Prime Directive always presupposes the technological superiority of the Federation. In a galaxy increasingly full of equals the days of the Prime Directive may be numbered, and tellingly, far fewer episodes of *Deep Space Nine* deal with the interpretation and application of the Directive. The *Star Trek* universe is again changing.

Some of these changes can be seen even more clearly in *Star Trek: Voyager,* the newest of the *Star Trek* series. Like *Deep Space Nine,* the crew of the *Voyager* is thrust into a world in which the old rules don't seem to apply, but here the situation is even more extreme. The ship, which was caught in a wild plasma storm, has been transported to the Delta Quadrant, an area of the galaxy some 75,000 light-years from home. *Voyager* has effectively no contact with the Federation, and so must address every value of the Federation anew in almost every episode. Like Commander Sisko, Captain Kathryn Janeway is presented with the task of upholding Federation values in a universe in which those values may no longer apply. She finds that she must forge an alliance with the Maquis, Federation enemies in her home quadrant. In the original series and in *The Next Generation* Captain Kirk and Captain Picard are both animated by a sense of the essential rightness of their position and judgment; they nearly always do the right thing and are vindicated in the end. But both Sisko and Janeway are presented with situations in which the old Federation ideas of right and wrong no longer exactly apply. The *Star Trek* universe of *Deep Space Nine* and *Voyager* is a considerably more ambiguous universe.

This ambiguity, and its corresponding lack of clear choices, can be seen in an episode of *Voyager* called "Tuvix." This episode begins with yet another transporter accident. As I said earlier, transporter accidents almost always bring up questions of character and identity, and "Tuvix" is no exception. Here the transporter merges Tuvok, the Vulcan science officer and security chief, and Neelix, the cook and morale officer. The resultant being takes the name Tuvix and immediately begins to sort out his identity. But by the time he begins to become a truly discrete individual, a true combination of Tuvok and Neelix, Janeway and the holographic doctor manage to discover how to separate the two. The problem now is that Tuvix has actually become an autonomous living being who sees the separation as a death sentence. He pleads for his own life, and in the end is ordered to subject himself to the separation. The final scene of the episode is truly remarkable, for it shows the only execution carried out by the Federation in all of *Star Trek*. Captain Janeway carries out what is tantamount to capital punishment. Tuvix regards it as such and fights for his life until the very end. So does the holographic doctor, who refuses to carry out the medical procedure necessary to separate the two characters on the grounds that it violates his Hippocratic oath not to take life. The other crew members look on in stunned silence as Janeway, a trained scientist, takes the controls and performs the procedure herself. To its credit, the episode looks unflinchingly at her action and does not attempt to gloss it over with any form of justification. We see the execution; we see Janeway leaving sickbay, troubled by what she has done; then we see *Voyager* rushing through space. She has made a difficult choice between two undesirable alternatives, and now she must learn to live with the choice. Nevertheless a death has cast a shadow over the ship, and for the first time in the series the Federation has put to death one of its own.

The *Star Trek* universe, of course, has always been full of alternate universes, and in a certain sense the two new series are showing us more of them. But episodes featuring alternate universes always end with a restoration of the barriers between the universe and a return of each universe's inhabitants to their rightful places. The new series are much more intent on disturbing the universe. The positions of things are disrupted and not always restored.

There is the very real possibility that the Klingons might go to war with the Federation or that *Voyager* might never return home to the Alpha Quadrant. One great strength of the *Star Trek* universe is the fact that it does not remain static, but there is an element of weakness in this as well. Like most balances of power, the balance of power seen in *The Next Generation* cannot last indefinitely. The *Star Trek* universe is a universe in flux, and part of the continuing appeal of the series is that the Federation and the ordered world it represents are not permanent institutions. An alternate universe episode of the original series, "Mirror, Mirror," posits a universe in which the Federation has become a totalitarian state. "Preemptive Strike" shows the Federation tending in that direction. But anything might happen, for the *Star Trek* universe is full not only of human disturbances, such as wars and rebellions, but of natural disturbances, such as anomalies, singularities, and fluctuations. Commander Sisko and Captain Janeway represent different responses to this changing universe, a universe in which one day, inevitably, there will be a whole new political landscape. The starship *Enterprise* is well named. An enterprise is a bold and imaginative undertaking, a willingness to undertake ventures of great scope, complication, and risk. When the challenges come to another generation of Starfleet officers, as come they will, the enterprise that is the United Federation of Planets will be ready to adapt and change, boldly going where no man has gone before.

ACKNOWLEDGMENTS

I would like to thank my editor, Bruce Tracy, and his assistant, Eliza Truitt. Thanks to my parents, Joan and Thomas Richards, for keeping their television tuned to *Star Trek* for so many hours. Special thanks to my agent, Chris Calhoun, not only for finding just the right publisher for *The Meaning of Star Trek* but for helping me think out the book in its early stages. This book is dedicated to my wife, Page Richards, who has spent thousands of hours by my side, watching *Star Trek*.